Twice-Exceptional Kids

*A Guide for Assisting Students Who Are Both
Academically Gifted and Learning Disabled*

Rosemary Callard-Szulgit

ROWMAN & LITTLEFIELD EDUCATION
Lanham • New York • Toronto • Plymouth, UK

Published in the United States of America
by Rowman & Littlefield Education
A division of Rowman & Littlefield Publishers, Inc.
A wholly owned subsidiary of The Rowman & Littlefield Publishing Group, Inc.
4501 Forbes Boulevard, Suite 200, Lanham, Maryland 20706
www.rowmaneducation.com

Estover Road, Plymouth PL6 7PY, United Kingdom

British Library Cataloguing in Publication Information Available

Library of Congress Cataloging-in-Publication Data
Callard-Szulgit, Rosemary, 1946-
    Twice-exceptional kids : a guide for assisting students who are both
academically gifted and learning disabled / Rosemary Callard-Szulgit.
        p. cm.
    Includes bibliographical references.
    ISBN-13: 978-1-57886-778-3 (cloth : alk. paper)
    ISBN-10: 1-57886-778-9 (cloth : alk. paper)
    ISBN-13: 978-1-57886-779-0 (pbk. : alk. paper)
    ISBN-10: 1-57886-779-7 (pbk. : alk. paper)
    1. Gifted children—Education—United States. 2. Learning disabled
children—Education—United States. I. Title.
LC3993.9.C354 2008
371.95—dc22

                                                              2007051462

⊗™ The paper used in this publication meets the minimum requirements of
American National Standard for Information Sciences—Permanence of Paper
for Printed Library Materials, ANSI/NISO Z39.48-1992.
Manufactured in the United States of America.

To be nobody else but yourself in a world that is constantly doing its best, night and day, to make you everybody else, is to fight the hardest battle you will ever fight, and never stop fighting.

—E. E. Cummings

I was humbled while researching and writing this book. Under the best of circumstances, life can be hard on a child. I can only imagine one's frustration with having a gifted intellect and then the inability to project that intellect successfully due to one or more learning disabilities.

I dedicate this book to all the courageous twice-exceptional children in our schools, their parents, their teachers, their classmates, and friends. May this book help you all with discovery, success, and life-fulfillment.

~

Contents

Preface

The special education needs of our nation's children continue to increase at alarmingly rapid rates every year. Equally alarming is the un-
derserving of our twice-exceptional (2E) children, who are not being adequately identified or understood, causing many 2Es to underachieve,
develop behavior problems, and either drop out of the system or fail.

This past semester, two of my graduate students were certified special education teachers, noted for being top-notch educators in their
schools. Our third class was focused on the twice exceptional. After I
completed my Power Point and opened the class up for discussion, both
special education teachers admitted they had never even heard the
term *twice exceptional*, nor had any of the other graduate students or
teachers. That evening's topic was an eye opener for everyone!

It doesn't take much imagination to understand why children who
are intellectually gifted but have one or more learning disabilities ham-
pering their success in school would have low self-esteem and high frustration levels. Many twice-exceptional children continue to fall through
the cracks in general education as well as special education classrooms.
Unfortunately, students often have to fail and/or achieve significantly
below their peers before they can receive specialized services by properly
trained teachers. Even then, remediation isn't always successful for the

2E children when curriculum and instructional levels are not adjusted for their higher intelligence. Boredom and frustration continue for these children.

Brody and Mills suggest there are three groups of learning-disabled gifted students who are likely to go unrecognized in our schools.[1] The first group of children has been identified as gifted but has been able to compensate well enough to avoid a diagnosis as learning disabled. As academic work becomes more challenging, their work begins to suffer and the system fails to test for a disability as an underlying cause for the 2E's poor performance.

Second are the gifted students whose learning disabilities are severe enough to classify them as being impaired, but whose intellectual giftedness is overlooked. These students may receive learning-disability services but do not receive instruction at the appropriate advanced levels.

Third are the children whose gifted aptitude and learning disabilities mask each other. Their cognitive giftedness is not recognized, and nor are their disabilities. It becomes an academic wash. These 2Es usually perform at grade level or slightly above.

As parents, teachers, and college students read this book, they will be better able to understand the twice exceptional, identify them in our schools, assess their needs, provide alternative models of instruction, find supportive counseling, and focus on the 2Es' intellectual gifts while helping them adjust with their learning disabilities.

Oh, my . . . what gifts we have to give them!

Note

1. L. E. Brody and C. J. Mills, "Gifted Children with Learning Disabilities: A Review of the Issues." *Journal of Learning Disabilities* 30 (1997): 282–97.

Introduction

I saw the angel in the marble.
All I did was set it free.

—Michelangelo

Many times I hear a parent or teacher say, "He may be gifted, but . . ." and the speaker continues with a focus on the child's weaknesses. In the educational realm of gifted children, many and various myths exist and are perpetuated. Even less understood is the twice-exceptional child, one who has a high level of intelligence but is hindered by learning, communication, and/or behavioral disabilities. Underachievement is often a result.

If we as parents or teachers are initially frustrated with the twice-exceptional child's lack of progress, imagine his or her frustration, being able to think well beyond his or her peers, yet unable to perform at the same high-ability level!

We can help the twice-exceptional child better succeed in two ways. First, we need to find out what his or her disability(ies) are and understand how they manifest themselves as interfering factors in his or her learning. We can then develop a support plan to help the child modify his or her processing and product.

Second, it is critically important to keep a focus on the twice-exceptional child's strengths. An intellectually gifted child often tends to be a perfectionist, being highly critical of himself or herself. Add to this the additional burden of disabilities interfering with the output of his or her high intelligence—the frustration can be overwhelming. Focusing on strengths rather than weaknesses is a powerful tool for all of us to use with any child.

I recently attended a special education parent-support meeting hosted by the state-appointed special education director. The parents had the pleasure of hearing the state superintendent of education speak and graciously answer their questions. I knew the superintendent had long been openly and politically supportive of gifted children's education rights in his state. He also supported the rights and appropriate education for special education children.

When my turn came to speak, I started with unquestioned praise for the superintendent's continued support of gifted children and their education, knowing that what works for gifted children works for all children. My question was, "What was being done for the gifted population children, twice-exceptional? Staff development opportunities? Parent training?"

His response was, "The focus of this meeting is special education, not gifted."

I'm sure the superintendent's special education director promptly filled him in after the meeting.

I'm pointing this example out to emphasize our need to continue educating everyone on the twice exceptional, students who are considered to be intellectually gifted in one or more areas and are also identified with a disability defined by federal and/or state eligibility criteria.

Twice-exceptional children (2Es) exist in all of our school districts. Their numbers are increasing every year. Perhaps part of the reason is we are becoming better able to identify and recognize 2Es through better identification procedures.

Can you imagine having an IQ of 145, able to think and achieve four or five years beyond your grade-level peers, yet failing because your thought processing takes longer than the allotted thirty-minute timed test?

Imagine parents' frustration, thinking their supposedly very bright child isn't really trying to succeed in school and not really knowing the child's handicapping condition(s) or how to adequately help him. Explaining the gifted child's academic test results and how the child excels, where his or her strengths abound, is a start! Equally important is an explanation of the 2E's learning disability, giving examples of how it might interfere with the child's thought-processing, social relationships, test taking, and/or ability to learn. Once the parents of a twice-exceptional child better understand the reasons for their child's lack of success in school, we can move forward with a more proactive talent development for the child.

Throughout my career, I have advocated for the rights of gifted children, emphasizing that what works for gifted children works for all children. As we continue to educate our current teachers, parents, and aspiring educators in the needs of gifted children and special education students, we can begin to free our twice-exceptional children from their encasement in the marble block of being unidentified and misunderstood.

May all children be free!

Regards,
Rosemary

~

Why a Bee?

Once upon a time the animals had a school. They had four subjects: running, climbing, flying, and swimming, and all animals took all subjects.

The duck was good at swimming, better than the teachers in fact. He made passing grades in running and flying, but he was almost hopeless in climbing. So they made him drop swimming to practice more climbing. Soon he was only average in swimming. But average is OK, and nobody worried much about it except the duck.

The eagle was considered a troublemaker. In his climbing class he beat everybody to the top of the tree, but he had his own way of getting there, which was against the rules. He always had to stay after school and write "Cheating is wrong" 500 times. This kept him from soaring, which he loved. But schoolwork comes first.

The bear flunked because they said he was lazy, especially in winter. His best time was summer, but school wasn't open then.

The penguin never went to school because he couldn't leave home, and they wouldn't start a school where he lived.

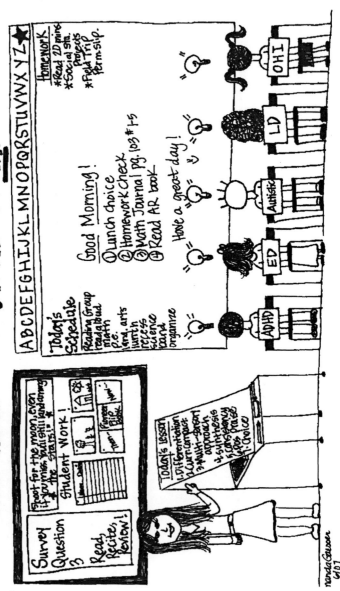

The zebra played hooky—a lot. The ponies made fun of his stripes, and that made him very sad.

The kangaroo started out at the top of the running class but got discouraged trying to run on all fours like the other kids.

The fish quit school because he was bored. To him, all four subjects were the same, but nobody understood that. They had never been a fish.

The squirrel got A's in climbing, but his flying teacher made him start from the ground up instead of the treetop down. His legs got so sore from practicing takeoffs that he began getting C's and D's in running.

But the bee was the biggest problem of all, so the teacher sent him to Dr. Owl for testing. Dr. Owl said that the bee's wings were just too small for flying, and besides they were in the wrong place. But the bee never saw Dr. Owl's report, so he just went ahead and flew anyway.

I think I know a bee or two, don't you?

(Author Unknown)

CHAPTER ONE

~

Who Are the Twice Exceptional?

As recently as yesterday, I was talking to a parent who assumed she had a clear understanding of what gifted children were like. I was amazed, as once again I was hearing various myths that continue to be portrayed as facts about gifted children. Gifted children are, by definition,

> children and youth with outstanding talent who perform or show the potential for performing at remarkably high levels of accomplishment when compared with others of their age, experience or environment. These children and youth exhibit high-performance capability in intellectual, creative and/or artistic areas, possess an unusual leadership capacity, or excel in specific academic fields. They require services or activities not ordinarily provided by the school.[1]

I actually require my graduate students to memorize this definition the first week of class so they will always be prepared to "set the record straight" whenever they are in earshot of inaccurate information being discussed by colleagues and /or parents.

Equally important to recognize and understand are the children we recognize as twice exceptional (2E).

Twice-exceptional students are

> students who are identified as gifted and talented in one or more areas of exceptionality (specific academics, general intellectual ability, creativity, leadership, visual, spatial, or performing arts) and also identified with a disability defined by Federal/State eligibility criteria, such as: perceptual communicative disability (learning disability), significant identifiable emotional disability, physical disabilities, sensory disabilities (visual, hearing), autism, or ADHD. Such a disability would qualify the twice-exceptional student for an Individual Education Plan (IEP) and/or a 504 Plan.[2]

The twice exceptional are gifted children who have the potential to perform well beyond the norm of their peers, yet are not succeeding in school due to one or more learning disabilities, masking and/or confusing their true abilities, frustrating the children, their parents, and oftentimes their teachers.

Twice-exceptional children are also asynchronous learners who are considered intelligent but are often not succeeding in school. During their primary years, many of these students have been able to succeed due to their superior intelligence. Eventually, the child's high intelligence can no longer compensate for his disability and school success begins to falter. Coupled with this is a rising frustration for the child, often leading to defensive behaviors, lack of interest, and social misconduct.

Learning disability is a general term that describes specific kinds of learning problems. A learning disability can cause a person to have trouble learning and using certain skills. The skills most often affected are: reading, writing, listening, speaking, reasoning, and doing math.

Learning disabilities are very common. As many as one out of every five people in the United States has a learning disability. Twice-exceptional children may be able to compensate for their disabilities for several years. Eventually, behaviors and school successes start to change. Teachers and parents notice the child is not learning as expected.

Some common characteristics to consider when assessing if your child may be twice exceptional and requiring special education services are:

- A noticeable difference between how well a child does in school and how well he or she could do, given his or her intelligence or ability.
- Cognitive processing deficit, which usually interferes with reading.
- May have memory problems.
- May be very independent in some areas, very dependent on adults where disability is involved.
- Can be very stubborn and inflexible.
- Unwilling to take risks in school-related areas, yet almost reckless outside of school.
- May not know where to begin a task or how to go on from there.
- May have high verbal ability but struggle to express ideas in writing.
- May have trouble understanding jokes, comic strips, and sarcasm.
- May not follow the social rules of conversation, such as taking turns, and may stand too close to the listener.
- Lack of appropriate social and emotional exchange.
- Poor relationships with classmates due to poor socialization skills.
- May have trouble following directions.
- Highly sensitive to criticism.
- Special talents or consuming interest.
- Discrepancies between student conceptualizations and actual production.
- Highly verbal yet often unable or unwilling to complete written assignments.
- Excelling at hands-on activities, but does not participate in classroom discussions and group activities.
- Divergent thinking to an extreme.
- Acting out behaviors, often signaling frustration in school.

Once your twice-exceptional child is diagnosed, special education and related support services will be an important part of his schooling. Before diagnosis, compensation strategies helped him succeed. With increased demands, especially in reading and writing, his one or more learning disabilities can't be completely compensated for simply by superior intelligence. Specific interventions and special education services will be important sources of help to your child and you. An individualized education program (IEP) will be developed by the school staff and you. This IEP will describe your child's unique needs and also describe the specific special education services that will be provided to meet those needs. These services will be provided at no cost to the child or family. The use of Plan 504 and other less formal plans are also available. A 504 Plan is a design of instructional services assisting students with special education needs who are in a regular classroom setting. This is distinct from an IEP, which is required for special education students who need significant remediation. More information about an IEP and Plan 504 is included in the appendix.

It became very clear during the research for this book that the greatest disservice we do to twice-exceptional children is focus on their deficits through remediation rather than focus on their strength, primarily intellectual giftedness. Curriculum is generally based on grade-level requirements, with little or no regard to acceleration, enrichment, and higher-order thinking skills.

As we continue to learn, focusing on best practices and strength-based instruction, our twice-exceptional children will prosper, as will all children. We do know that the following activities work for all children:

- Teaching creative problem solving
- Teaching higher-level thinking skills
- Teaching conflict resolution skills
- Encouragement, patience, and understanding
- High standards
- Fair discipline and consequences
- Teaching healthy and positive choices
- Providing alternative methods of instruction and product selection
- Chances for enrichment and acceleration
- Making use of assistive technology
- Teaching and supporting study skills and time management
- Providing clear and fair evaluation/grading rubrics

The chapters that follow give overviews of the common learning disabilities affecting twice-exceptional children, with suggested tips for parents and teachers. While emotional disturbance is not included in the federal law of learning disability, I have included it as a learning guide for the reader. If you see recognizable signs, I hope the information and suggestions I've included can help you with the appropriate steps and guidelines to follow. States may vary in what they do and do not support as defined learning disabilities, but must stay within the federal guidelines of the law.

I wish you well on this journey. We all are here to help each other. I look forward to helping you.

Notes

1. P. Ross, ed., *National Excellence: A Case for Developing America's Talent.* Washington, DC: U.S. Government Printing Office, 1993, 26.

2. *Twice-Exceptional Students: Gifted Students with Disabilities: An Introductory Resource Book.* Denver, Colorado: Colorado Department of Education, n.d., 9.

CHAPTER TWO

~

Models of Service for the Twice-Exceptional Student

According to federal definition 34 CFR 300.550, each state education agency shall provide a least-restrictive environment for special education students. To this end, inclusion classrooms have been created to ensure, to the maximum extent appropriate, that children with disabilities, including children in public or private institutions or other care facilities, are educated with children who are nondisabled.

The placement of students with disabilities in a least-restrictive environment shall:

- provide the special education needed by the student,
- provide for education of the student to the maximum extent appropriate to the needs of the student with other students who do not have disabilities, and
- be as close as possible to the student's home.

One result of the Individuals with Disabilities Act (Public Law 105-17) is the placement of identified special education children in the general education classroom. It is always the goal to service twice-exceptional and all special education students in the least-restrictive environment. Following are examples of four service models ranging from least restrictive to most restrictive that parents and schools may consider for 2E student placement.

Inclusion in the regular education classroom with gifted and Learning Resource Center consult only. This least-restrictive education model requires the classroom teacher to meet the differentiated needs of all academic levels of children within her classroom during the school day. The consultant for gifted services can help by differentiating units of instruction for the teacher and also help develop compacted units of instruction for the gifted students above grade level as well as for children below grade level norms. The Learning Resource Center consult can do the same in addition to gathering materials of instruction and any other helpful education tools of instruction.

Inclusion in the regular education classroom with pull-out for Learning Resource Center and gifted classes. This model of instruction finds the twice-exceptional student going to a Learning Resource Center (classroom) within the school for a specified amount of time each day for one or more days a week. The Resource Center teacher follows the individualized education program (IEP) of the twice-exceptional child, focusing on his strengths for talent development and using alternative learning strategies to help him achieve at his advanced level of aptitude.

2E self-contained classroom in the student's home school district. A classroom designed for twice-exceptional students who have not been successful at accessing accelerated and enriched instruction in less restrictive environments in their educational setting will have a curriculum addressing the academic, social/emotional, and remedial needs of the children. The student-to-teacher ratio should be consistent with class sizes of other self-contained programs. The program will provide the students with adaptations, accommodations, and special instruction that enable these gifted, learning-disabled children access to a more appropriate and rigorous curriculum than their grade-level peers. The 2E classroom setting should provide students with strength-based instruction and utilize a higher level of thinking skills—best practices for all children!

Private placement. The most restrictive environment would be placement at a private school setting not affiliated with the student's home school district.

Inclusive education is:

- Attending your home school and/or having the same choices as other students
- Full participation in all aspects of your school
- Access to specific special education services within the general education framework
- Learning with your peers, even if you have different educational goals
- Ongoing and realistic support for your teachers with adequate preparation and staff development resources
- Healthy and positive interactions and relationships in the school environment
- Ongoing problem solving with your teachers to assist you with your education and social interactions

Inclusive education is not:

- One size fits all
- "Visiting" general education classes
- Here today—gone tomorrow
- Servicing students without adequate teacher training and education
- Placement of students in general education classroom settings without ongoing support for teacher(s) and students(s)
- Denying differences exist

CHAPTER THREE

~

Asperger's Syndrome

Bobby's Story

When Bobby was four years old, his baby sister was born. While his parents and relatives all seemed very happy with Sonja's arrival, Bobby clearly was not! He began to have mini temper tantrums, did not want to share his parents' time with Sonja, and clearly was not loving and affectionate toward his new sister. At first, everyone pretty much assumed Bobby had a strong case of sibling rivalry. The following year when Bobby entered kindergarten, his teachers noticed aggressive outbursts regularly from him. He became verbally argumentative with his parents, teachers, and other adults in his life. Bobby also seemed to be hyperactive. Bobby's parents still thought his problematic behavior was a result of their daughter's birth, but his teachers were more concerned with a possible neurological disorder. Bobby's parents agreed to have him tested by the school psychologist. He was diagnosed with Asperger's Syndrome (AS). Due to immediate and effective interventions by his parents, teachers, and other significant adults, Bobby is now a productive and successful second grader.

Asperger's Syndrome Defined

Coupled with myths surrounding gifted children, there seems to be growing confusion about gifted children with Asperger's Syndrome and twice-exceptional children. There has been tremendous interest and a surge of research about AS in the past five years, but giftedness is rarely mentioned.[1]

Author C. Little helps clear up some of the common misunderstandings and confusion between gifted traits and Asperger's Syndrome traits:

Asperger's Syndrome
- Advanced vocabulary
- Unaware of another's perspective
- Literal thought
- Poor language comprehension
- Intensity of focus
- Introverted
- Excellent memory
- Sensory sensitivity

Gifted
- Advanced vocabulary
- Ability to see another's viewpoint
- High abstract thinking skills
- Good language comprehension
- Intensity of focus
- Introverted
- Excellent memory
- Sensitivity toward others

Twice-Exceptional
- Advanced vocabulary
- Unaware of another's perspective
- Intensity of focus
- Sensory sensitivity
- Introverted

- Enjoys "rote" exercises
- Poor language comprehension[2]

The author does note that there are many commonalities between the lists and the reader should note what motivation is behind each behavior. If you review Little's lists, you'll note a distinction between a child with an advanced vocabulary who is unaware of another's perspective and a child with an advanced vocabulary and the ability to see another's viewpoint. Literal thought is certainly different from high abstract thinking skills.

Asperger's Syndrome is defined by Goldberg-Edelson as follows:

For this diagnosis to be made, there must be qualitative impairment in social interaction as manifested by at least two of the following: marked impairment in the use of multiple nonverbal behaviors (e.g., eye contact, gestures); failure to develop age appropriate peer relationships; lack of spontaneous seeking to share interest or achievements with others; lack of spontaneous achievements with others; lack of social or emotional reciprocity; restricted repetitive and stereotyped patterns of behaviors, interests and activities as manifested by at least one of the following: preoccupation with at least one stereotyped and restricted pattern of interest to an abnormal degree; inflexible adherence to nonfunctional routines or rituals; stereotyped and repetitive motor mannerisms; and preoccupation with parts of objects. There must additionally be clinically significant impairment in social occupational or other functioning; and clinically significant delay in language cognitive development, adaptive behavior, or in curiosity about the environment.[3]

It is generally thought that Asperger's Syndrome appears to run in families, with more boys being diagnosed than girls. Developmental delays, impairment of social reciprocity, anxiety related to small changes, and trouble seeing the bigger picture and immaturity are often clear, recognizable symptoms. However, both gifted children with and without AS can give great attention and focus to creative topics and items of interest.

I feel it is critical to clear up some of the misunderstandings coupling gifted and AS children so that gifted children are not simply lumped into a special education label, which seems to be currently happening in many educational settings.

One of my friends has a wonderfully gifted four-year-old son who is currently being treated for AS. What I find astonishing is that my friend was told by his son's psychologist that 80 percent of gifted children have Asperger's. I was so angered when I heard that statistic quoted, I asked for the documentation and research to validate that statement. We have never received copies of such research, and I have encouraged my friend to find a different psychologist!

Tips for Parents and Teachers

- Help children with AS set goals, short and long term while routinely checking in with them so the children don't lose sight of their importance. They'll also need help prioritizing.
- To help with time management, set up a calendar with the children showing daily, weekly, and monthly tasks and assignments. Having a visual cue helps the children better define timelines and not become overwhelmed with too many thoughts/tasks at once.
- Consequences need to be related as sequential and specific to the act.
- Talk about common school and social activities, discussing appropriate behaviors and responses. Role play. Look for commonalities.
- Try to keep homework and evening assignments to a minimum, as the children may well have expended their energy and focus during the day.
- Helping children prioritize the relative importance of tasks and appropriate amounts of time to spend on them is huge. This needs to be done regularly.
- Remembering to focus on the 2E's high intellect with acceleration, differentiation, and independent study, as long as study habits are closely monitored, it is truly a positive and proactive approach with twice exceptional children and AS. Primarily focusing on 2E children's disabilities with remediation without

highlighting and working with their intellectual giftedness is tantamount to education sacrilege.

Notes

1. See A. Cash, "A Profile of Gifted Individuals with Autism: The Twice-Exceptional Learner." *Roeper Review* 22 (1999): 22–27; and A. Cash, "Autism: The Silent Mask," in *The Many Faces of Giftedness*, ed. A. Y. Baldwin and W. Vialle, 209–38 (Albany, NY: Wadsworth Publishing, 1999).

2. C. Little, "Which Is It? Asperger's Syndrome or Giftedness: Defining the Differences." *Gifted Child Today* (Winter 2002): 58–63.

3. M. Goldberg-Edelson, "Autism-Related Disorders in DSM-IV," Center for the Student of Autism website, www.autism.org/dms.html (accessed March 22, 2001).

CHAPTER FOUR

~

Attention-Deficit/
Hyperactivity Disorder (AD/HD)

Mario's Story

Mario is ten years old. When he was seven, his family learned he had Attention-Deficit/Hyperactivity Disorder (AD/HD). At the time, he was driving everyone crazy. At school, he couldn't stay in his seat or keep quiet. At home, he didn't finish his homework or his chores. He did scary things, too, like climb out of his window onto the roof and run across the street without looking.

Things are much better now. Mario was tested by a trained professional to find out what he does well and what gives him trouble. His parents and teachers came up with ways to help him at school. Mario has trouble sitting still, so now he does some of his work standing up. He's also the student who tidies up the room and washes the chalkboard. His teachers break down his lessons into several parts. Then they have him do each part one at a time. This helps Mario keep his attention on his work.

At home, things have changed, too. Now his parents know why he's so active. They are careful to praise him when he does something well. They even have a reward program to encourage good behavior. He earns "good job points" that they post on a wall chart. After earning ten points he gets to choose something fun he'd like to do. Having a child with AD/HD is still a challenge, but things are looking better.

Attention-Deficit/Hyperactivity Disorder Defined

Attention-Deficit/Hyperactivity Disorder (AD/HD) is a condition that can make it hard for a person to sit still, control behavior, and pay attention. These difficulties usually begin before the person is seven years old. However, these behaviors may not be noticed until the child is older.

Doctors do not know just what causes AD/HD. However, researchers who study the brain are coming closer to understanding what may cause AD/HD. They believe that some people with AD/HD do not have enough of certain chemicals (called neurotransmitters) in their brain. These chemicals help the brain control behavior.

Parents and teachers do not cause AD/HD. Still there are many things that both parents and teachers can do to help a child with AD/HD.

As many as 5 out of every 100 children in school may have AD/HD. Boys are three times more likely than girls to have AD/HD.

There are three main signs, or symptoms, of AD/HD. These are:

- Problems with paying attention
- Being very active (called hyperactivity)
- Acting before thinking (called impulsivity)

More information about these symptoms is listed in a book called the *Diagnostic and Statistical Manual of Mental Disorders* (DSM), which is published by the American Psychiatric Association.[1] Based on these symptoms, three types of AD/HD have been found:

- *Inattentive* type, where the person can't seem to get focused or stay focused on a task or activity
- *Hyperactive-impulsive* type, where the person is very active and often acts without thinking
- *Combined* type, where the person is inattentive, impulsive, and too active

Inattentive type. Many children with AD/HD have problems paying attention. Children with the inattentive type of AD/HD often:

- do not pay close attention to details;
- can't stay focused on play or school work;
- don't follow through on instructions or finish school work or chores;
- can't seem to organize tasks and activities;
- get distracted easily.

Hyperactive-impulsive type. Being too active is probably the most visible sign of AD/HD. The hyperactive child is "always on the go." (As he or she gets older, the level of activity may go down.) These children also act before thinking (called *impulsivity*). For example, they may run across the road without looking or climb to the top of very tall trees. They may be surprised to find themselves in a dangerous situation. They may have no idea of how to get out of the situation.

Hyperactivity and impulsivity tend to go together. Children with the hyperactive-impulsive type of AD/HD often may:

- fidget and squirm;
- get out of their chairs when they're not supposed to;
- run around or climb constantly;
- have trouble playing quietly;
- talk too much;
- blurt out answers before questions have been completed;
- have trouble waiting their turn;
- interrupt others when they're talking.

Combined type. Children with the combined type of AD/HD have symptoms of both of the types described above. They have problems with paying attention, with hyperactivity, and with controlling their impulses.

Of course from time to time, all children are inattentive, impulsive, and too active. With children who have AD/HD, *these behaviors are the rule, not the exception.*

These behaviors can cause a child to have real problems at home, at school, and with friends. As a result, many children with AD/HD will feel anxious, unsure of themselves, and depressed. These feelings are not symptoms of AD/HD. They come from having problems again and again at home and in school.

When a child shows signs of AD/HD, he or she needs to be evaluated by a trained professional. This person may work for the school system or may be a professional in private practice. A complete evaluation is the only way to know for sure if the child has AD/HD. It is also important to:

- rule out other reasons for the child's behavior; and
- find out if the child has other disabilities along with AD/HD.

There is no quick treatment of AD/HD. However, the symptoms of AD/HD can be managed. It's important that the child's family and teachers:

- find out more about AD/HD;
- create an educational program that fits the child's individual needs; and
- provide medication if parents and the doctor feel this would help the child.

School can be hard for children with AD/HD. Success in school often means being able to pay attention and control behavior and impulse. These are the areas where children with AD/HD have trouble.

There are many ways the school can help students with AD/HD. Some students may be eligible to receive special education services under the Individuals with Disabilities Education Act (IDEA). Under the newest amendments to IDEA, passed in 1997, AD/HD is specifically mentioned under the category of "Other Health Impairment" (OHI). Other students will not be eligible for services under IDEA. However, they may be eligible for services under a different law, Section 504 of the Rehabilitation Act of 1973. In both cases, the school and the child's parents need to meet and talk about what special help the student needs.

Most students with AD/HD are helped by supports or changes in the classroom (called *adaptations*).

Tips for Parents

- Learn about AD/HD. The more you know, the more you can help yourself and your child.
- Praise your child when he or she does well. Build your child's abilities. Talk about and encourage his or her strengths and talents.
- Be clear, be consistent, be positive. Set clear rules for your child. Tell your child what he or she *should* do, not just what he shouldn't do. Be clear about what will happen if your child does not follow the rules. Have a reward program for good behavior. Praise your child when he or she shows the behaviors you like.
- Learn about strategies for managing your child's behavior. These include valuable techniques such as: charting, having a reward program, ignoring behaviors, natural consequences, logical consequences, and time-out. Using these strategies will lead to more positive behaviors and cut down on problem behaviors. You can read about these techniques in many books. See "Suggested Readings" at the end of this book.
- Talk with your doctor about whether medication will help your child.
- Pay attention to your child's mental health (and your own!). Be open to counseling. It can help you deal with the challenges of raising a child with AD/HD. It can help your child deal with frustration, feel better about himself or herself, and learn more about social skills.
- Talk to other parents whose children have AD/HD. Parents can share practical advice and emotional support.
- Meet with the school and develop an educational plan to address your child's needs. Both you and your child's teachers should get a written copy of this plan.
- Keep in touch with your child's teacher. Tell the teacher how your child is doing at home. Ask how your child is doing in school. Offer support.

Tips for Teachers

- Learn more about AD/HD.
- Figure out what specific things are hard for the student. For example, one student with AD/HD may have trouble starting a task, while another may have trouble ending one task and starting the next. Each student needs different help.
- Post rules, schedules, and assignments. Clear rules and routines will help a student with AD/HD. Have set times for specific tasks. Call attention to changes in the schedule.
- Show the student how to use an assignment book and a daily schedule. Also teach study skills and learning strategies, and reinforce these regularly.
- Help the student channel his or her physical activity (e.g., let the student do some work standing up or at the board). Provide regularly scheduled breaks.
- Make sure directions are given step-by-step, and that the student is following the directions. Give directions both verbally and in writing. Many students with AD/HD also benefit from doing the steps as separate tasks.
- Let the student do work on a computer.
- Work together with the student's parents to create and implement an educational plan tailored to meet the student's needs. Regularly share information about how the student is doing at home and at school.
- Have high expectations for the student, but be willing to try new ways of doing things. Be patient. Maximize the student's chances for success.[2]

Notes

1. American Psychiatric Association, *Diagnostic and Statistical Manual of Mental Disorders* (DSM-IV-TR), 4th ed. rev. (Washington, DC: American Psychiatric Association, 2000).

2. Special thanks to NICHCY (National Dissemination Center for Children with Disabilities) Fact Sheet #19, www.nichcy.org.

CHAPTER FIVE

~

Autism/PDD

Ryan's Story

Ryan is a healthy, active two-year-old, but his parents are concerned because he doesn't seem to be doing the same things that his older sister did at this age. He's not really talking yet, although sometimes he repeats, over and over, words that he hears others say. He doesn't use words to communicate, though. It seems he just enjoys the sounds of them. Ryan spends a lot of time playing by himself. He has a few favorite toys, mostly cars, or anything with wheels on it! And sometimes, he spins himself around as fast as he does the wheels on his cars. Ryan's parents are really concerned, as he's started throwing a tantrum whenever his routine has the smallest change. More and more, his parents feel stressed, not knowing what might trigger Ryan's next upset.

Often, it seems Ryan doesn't notice or care if his family or anyone else is around. His parents just don't know how to reach their little boy, who seems so rigid and far too set in his ways for his tender young age. After talking with their family doctor, Ryan's parents call the Early Intervention office in their community and make an appointment to have Ryan evaluated.

Ryan is seen by several professionals who play with him, watch him, and ask his parents a lot of questions. When they're all done, Ryan is diagnosed with a form of autism. As painful as this is for his parents to learn, the early intervention staff try to encourage them. By getting an early diagnosis and beginning treatment, Ryan has the best chance to grow and develop. Of course, there's a long road ahead, but his parents take comfort in knowing that they aren't alone and they're getting Ryan the help he needs.

Autism and Pervasive Development Disorder Defined

Autism and Pervasive Development Disorder–NOS (not otherwise specified) are developmental disabilities that share many of the same characteristics. Usually evident by age three, autism and PDD-NOS are neurological disorders that affect a child's ability to communicate, understand language, play, and relate to others.

In the diagnostic manual used to classify disabilities, the DSM-IV, "autistic disorder" is listed as a category under the heading of "Pervasive Developmental Disorders."[1] A diagnosis of autistic disorder is made when an individual displays six or more of twelve symptoms listed across three major areas: social interaction, communication, and behavior. When children display similar behaviors but do not meet the criteria for autistic disorder, they may receive a diagnosis referred to as PDD-NOS; throughout the remainder of this chapter, I will refer to the diagnosis as PDD, as it is more commonly known.

Autistic disorder is one of the disabilities specifically defined in the Individuals with Disabilities Education Act (IDEA), the federal legislation under which children and youth with disabilities receive special education and related services. IDEA, which uses the term "autism," defines the disorder as "a developmental disability significantly affecting verbal and nonverbal communication and social interaction, usually evident before age 3, that adversely affects a child's educational performance. Other characteristics often associated with autism are engagement in repetitive activities and stereotyped movements, resistance to environmental change or change in daily routines, and unusual responses to sensory experiences."

Due to the similarity of behaviors associated with autism and PDD, use of the term *pervasive developmental disorder* has caused some confusion among parents and professionals. However, the treatment and educational needs are similar for both diagnoses.

Autism and PDD occur in approximately 5 to 15 per 10,000 births. These disorders are four times more common in boys than in girls. The causes of autism and PDD are unknown. Currently, researchers are investigating areas such as neurological damage and biochemical imbalance in the brain. These disorders are not caused by psychological factors.

Characteristics

Some or all of the following characteristics may be observed in mild to severe forms:

- Communication problems (e.g., using and understanding language)
- Difficulty relating to people, objects, and events
- Unusual play with toys and other objects
- Difficulty with changes in routine or familiar surroundings
- Repetitive body movements or behavior patterns

Children with autism or PDD vary widely in abilities, intelligence, and behaviors. Some children do not speak; others have language that often includes repeated phrases or conversations. Persons with more advanced language skills tend to use a small range of topics and have difficulty with abstract concepts. Repetitive play skills, a limited range of interests, and impaired social skills are generally evident as well. Unusual responses to sensory information—for example, loud noises, lights, certain textures of food or fabrics—are also common.

Early diagnosis and appropriate educational programs are very important to children with autism or PDD. Public Law (P.L.) 105-17, the Individuals with Disabilities Education Act (IDEA), formerly P.L. 94-142, includes autism as a disability category. From the age of three, children with autism and PDD are eligible for educational programs appropriate to their individual needs. Educational programs for students with autism or PDD focus on improving communication and social, academic, behavioral, and daily living skills. Behavior and communication problems that interfere with learning sometimes require the assistance of a knowledgeable professional in the autism field who develops and helps to implement a plan that can be carried out at home and school.

The classroom environment should be structured so that the program is consistent and predictable. Students with autism or PDD learn better and are less confused when information is presented visually as well as verbally. Interaction with nondisabled peers is also important, for these students provide models of appropriate language, social, and behavioral skills. To overcome frequent problems in generalizing skills learned at school, it is very important to develop programs with parents so that learning activities, experiences, and approaches can be carried over into the home and community.

With educational programs designed to meet a student's individual needs and specialized adult support services in employment and living arrangements, many children and adults with autism or PDD grow up to live and work successfully in the community.

Tips for Parents

- Learn about autism/PDD. The more you know, the more you can help yourself and your child.
- Be mindful to interact with and teach your child in ways that are most likely to get a positive response. Learn what is likely to trigger melt-downs for your child, so you can try to minimize them. Remember, the earliest years are the toughest, but it does get better!
- Learn from professionals and other parents how to meet your child's special needs, but remember your son or daughter is first and foremost a child; life does not need to become a never-ending round of therapies.
- If you weren't born loving highly structured, consistent schedules and routines, ask for help from other parents and professionals on how to make it second nature for you. Behavior, communication, and social skills can all be areas of concern for a child with autism, and experience tells us that maintaining a solid, loving, and structured approach in caring for your child can help greatly.

- Learn about assistive technology that can help your child. This may include a simple picture communication board to help your child express needs and desires, or may be as sophisticated as an augmentative communication device.
- Work with professionals in early intervention or in your school to develop an individual family service plan (IFSP) or an individualized education program (IEP) that reflects your child's needs and abilities. Be sure to include related services, supplementary aids and services, assistive technology (AT), and a positive behavioral support plan, if needed.
- Be patient, and stay optimistic. Your child, like every child, has a whole lifetime to learn and grow.

Tips for Teachers

- Learn more about autism/PDD. Make sure directions are given step-by-step, verbally, visually, and by providing physical supports or prompts, as needed by the student. Students with autism spectrum disorders often have trouble interpreting facial expressions, body language, and tone of voice. Be as concrete and explicit as possible in your instructions and feedback to the student.
- Find out what the student's strengths and interests are and emphasize them. Tap into those avenues and create opportunities for success. Give positive feedback and lots of opportunities for practice.
- Build opportunities for the student to have social/collaborative interactions throughout the regular school day. Provide support, structure, and lots of feedback.
- If behavior is a significant issue for the student, seek help from expert professional resources (including parents) to understand the meanings of the behaviors and to develop a unified, positive approach to resolving them.
- Have consistent routines and schedules. When you know a change in routine will occur (e.g., a field trip or assembly) *prepare* the student by telling him or her what is going to be different and what to expect or do. Reward students for each small success.
- Work together with the student's parents and other school personnel to create and implement an educational plan tailored to

meet the student's needs. Regularly share information about how the student is doing at school and at home.[2]

Notes

1. American Psychiatric Association, *Diagnostic and Statistical Manual of Mental Disorders* (DSM-IV-TR), 4th ed. rev. (Washington, DC: American Psychiatric Association, 2000).

2. Special thanks to NICHCY (National Dissemination Center for Children with Disabilities) Fact Sheet #1, www.nichcy.org.

CHAPTER SIX

⌒

Deafness and Hearing Loss

The Individuals with Disabilities Education Act (IDEA), formerly the Education of the Handicapped Act (P.L. 94-142), includes "hearing impairment" and "deafness" as two of the categories under which children with disabilities may be eligible for special education and related services programming. While the term "hearing impairment" is often used generically to describe a wide range of hearing losses, including deafness, the regulations for IDEA define hearing loss and deafness separately.

Hearing impairment is defined by IDEA as "an impairment in hearing, whether permanent or fluctuating, that adversely affects a child's educational performance." Deafness is defined as "a hearing impairment that is so severe that the child is impaired in processing linguistic information through hearing, with or without amplification."

Thus, deafness may be viewed as a condition that prevents an individual from receiving sound in all or most of its forms. In contrast, a child with a hearing loss can generally respond to auditory stimuli, including speech.

Hearing loss and deafness affect individuals of all ages and may occur at any time from infancy through old age. The U.S. Department of Education reports that, during the 2000–2001 school year, 70,767 students

37

aged six to twenty-one (or 1.3 percent of all students with disabilities) received special education services under the category of "hearing impairment." However, the number of children with hearing loss and deafness is undoubtedly higher, since many of these students may have other disabilities as well and may be served under other categories.

School Environment (Educational Implications)

Hearing loss or deafness does not affect a person's intellectual capacity or ability to learn. However, children who are either hard of hearing or deaf generally require some form of special education services in order to receive an adequate education. Such services may include:

- regular speech, language, and auditory training from a specialist;
- amplification systems;
- services of an interpreter for those students who use sign language;
- favorable seating in the class to facilitate lip reading;
- captioned films/videos;
- assistance of a note taker, who takes notes for the student with a hearing loss, so that the student can fully attend to instruction;
- instruction for the teacher and peers in alternate communication methods, such as sign language; and
- counseling.

Children who are hard of hearing will find it much more difficult than children who have normal hearing to learn vocabulary, grammar, word order, idiomatic expressions, and other aspects of verbal communication. For children who are deaf or have severe hearing losses, early, consistent, and conscious use of visible communication modes (such as sign language, finger spelling, and cued speech) and/or amplification and aural/oral training can help reduce this language delay. By age four or five, most children who are deaf are enrolled in school on a full-day basis and do special work on communication and language development. It is important for teachers and audiologists to work together to teach the child to use his or her residual hearing to the maximum extent possible, even if the preferred means of communication is manual.

Since the great majority of deaf children (over 90 percent) are born to hearing parents, programs should provide instruction for parents on implications of deafness within the family. People with hearing loss use oral or manual means of communication or a combination of the two. Oral communication includes speech, lip reading, and the use of residual hearing. Manual communication involves signs and finger spelling. Total Communication, as a method of instruction, is a combination of the oral method plus signing and finger spelling.

Individuals with hearing loss, including those who are deaf, now have many helpful devices available to them. Text telephones (known as TTs, TTYs, or TDDs) enable persons to type phone messages over the telephone network. The Telecommunications Relay Service (TRS), now required by law, makes it possible for TT users to communicate with virtually anyone (and vice versa) via telephone. Dial 711 to access TRS anywhere in the United States. The relay service is free.[1]

Note

1. Special thanks to NICHCY (National Dissemination Center for Children with Disabilities) Fact Sheet #3, www.nichcy.org.

CHAPTER SEVEN

~

Dyslexia

Meghan's Story

Meghan was a bright, social, active four-year-old. She was able to recite stories she had listened to in books on tape. She could do many math problems in her head and was very verbal. Meghan's parents began to expose their daughter to primer books, expecting Meghan to read unendingly. When Meghan couldn't seem to decode easily, she became frustrated, a bit belligerent, and hostile toward her reading books. This was totally out of character for this bright, sweet young girl. From Meghan's parents' perspective, their daughter was a very bright and gifted young girl, yet, why couldn't she read commensurate with her other advanced abilities? Their doctor recommended taking Meghan to a health care professional specializing in learning disabilities. Meghan was diagnosed with dyslexia and is being treated for it, learning new ways to remember sounds, using a tape recorder in first grade for classroom lessons and homework assignments rather than the traditional reading and writing lessons—so far, so good. Meghan should be able to have many successful school years with tutors and teachers who understand her learning disability and are proactive with supportive learning aids and technology. Emotional support from everyone involved in her schooling will also be a big help to her.

Ine v er re a l l y und ers t oo d wh at is wa s lik e fo rach il dto l iv ewi thd yslex ia unt i l l d idre sea rc h fo rth i sbo ok!

Translation: I never really understood what it was like for a child to have dyslexia until I did research for this book! I was initially saddened and my heart seemed to go out to every child with this disability. As I continued my research and writing, I began to rally and reminded myself that helping gifted and all children with disabilities was exactly why I was writing this book, and to help their parents and teachers as well.

Dyslexia Defined

Dyslexia is a learning problem that interferes with a child's reading and writing. With dyslexia, messages in the brain can get mixed up or confused, making it difficult for a child to read and remember what he or she has read. Dyslexia can also be associated with difficulties in any or a number of the following areas:

- Handwriting
- Oral language
- Mathematics
- Motor planning and coordination
- Organization
- Sequencing
- Orientation to time
- Focus and attention
- Right-left orientation
- Spatial perception
- Auditory and visual processing
- Eye movement control
- Memory[1]

Once reading becomes an important part of the schoolwork, dyslexic children's struggles increase tremendously. If your young, intellectually gifted child has been progressing well beyond his age-group peers as a toddler and preschooler, seemingly very bright, then starts jumbling messages and confusing reading skills, you might well suspect dyslexia.

Most important is to have a qualified specialist meet with your child, provide a formal assessment, and prescribe best practices and interventions for your 2E child, you, and his teachers. It will also help you to become familiar with the behaviors of twice-exceptional students compared with the behaviors of others with the same disability.

Tips for Parents and Teachers

- A multisensory teaching approach is essential—helping a child to learn through more than one of the senses.
- Use flash cards for memory enhancement.
- Let the child record on tape or disk classroom lessons and assignments.
- Use special computer programs to help children sound out words.
- Provide ongoing emotional support.
- Remind them that Tom Cruise, Thomas Edison, and Walt Disney all succeeded in spite of being dyslexic!

Note

1. B. L. Eide and F. F. Eide, *The Mislabeled Child: How Understanding Your Child's Unique Learning Style Can Open the Door to Success* (New York: Hyperion, 2006).

CHAPTER EIGHT

~

Emotional Disturbance

Jamie's Story

Jamie was a twice-exceptional child, very gifted across the board, testing with an IQ of 145. He had been diagnosed as emotionally disturbed at the age of seven and placed in an 8:1:1 special education classroom in our elementary school. When Jamie was ready for fourth grade, his special education teacher believed Jamie could succeed in our self-contained classroom for gifted children. At that time, our district began services for identified gifted children in a self-contained fourth-grade classroom, busing the children throughout the district to a central location—my classroom.

Initially, Jamie's parents were both happy and worried when Jamie's teacher suggested he was progressing well enough to be mainstreamed and placed in a self-contained classroom for gifted children. We all agreed to start Jamie in my class, with bimonthly meetings to discuss Jamie's progress.

Jamie flourished immediately and became an academic and social star in our class. Three months into the school year, our class developed and produced a play based on the Aesop Fables. Jamie had one of the leading roles and performed magnificently.

45

What happened in the fourth month of school was very sad and perhaps, in retrospect, predictable. The school counselor, special education teacher, and I met with Jamie and his parents regularly to consult on Jamie's academic and emotional progress. The initial ED characteristic Jamie exemplified when diagnosed was that of immaturity—inappropriate crying, temper tantrums, and poor coping skills.

During our bimonthly meetings, Jamie's mother increasingly insisted that he was showing signs of tension, stress, unhappiness, and temper tantrums at home. We were seeing none of these behaviors in school. Jamie's mom started coming to school to make sure he was OK. Once he saw his mom at the classroom door, Jamie's calm and engaged behavior started becoming anxious, distressed, and disengaged. It became increasingly apparent that Jamie's mom needed him to be sick and at home with her. The fifth time his mom arrived at school to check up on him, Jamie had a breakdown. He started screaming, kicking, fighting, and shouting vulgarities. When the ambulance arrived, Jamie was put in a strait jacket and wheeled down the corridor with the school in a lockdown. Even with all the doors and windows closed, Jamie's terrorizing screams and demands of wanting to get back into his mother's womb pierced all of our ears for many years to follow.

I've included this case as a reminder to all of us in education. We can do our very best and give all that is possible to give and still have mitigating circumstances deny us success.

I never heard what happened to Jamie. His mom cut off all connection with our school, blamed us for his breakdown, and began home schooling. I can only hope that someday, somehow, this family can be well.

Emotional Disturbance Defined

Many terms are used to describe emotional, behavioral, or mental disorders. Currently, students with such disorders are categorized as having an emotional disturbance, which is defined under the Individuals with Disabilities Education Act as

> a condition exhibiting one or more of the following characteristics over a long period of time and to a marked degree that adversely affects a child's educational performance—

(A) An inability to learn that cannot be explained by intellectual, sensory, or health factors.

(B) An inability to build or maintain satisfactory interpersonal relationships with peers and teachers.

(C) Inappropriate types of behavior or feelings under normal circumstances.

(D) A general pervasive mood of unhappiness or depression.

(E) A tendency to develop physical symptoms or fears associated with personal or school problems.[1]

As defined by the IDEA, emotional disturbance includes schizophrenia but does not apply to children who are socially maladjusted, unless it is determined that they have an emotional disturbance.[2]

The causes of emotional disturbance have not been adequately determined. Although various factors such as heredity, brain disorder, diet, stress, and family functioning have been suggested as possible causes, research has not shown any of these factors to be the direct cause of behavior or emotional problems. Some of the characteristics and behaviors seen in children who have emotional disturbances include:

- hyperactivity (short attention span, impulsiveness);
- aggression/self-injurious behavior (acting out, fighting);
- withdrawal (failure to initiate interaction with others; retreat from exchanges of social interaction, excessive fear or anxiety);
- immaturity (inappropriate crying, temper tantrums, poor coping skills); and
- learning difficulties (academically performing below grade level).

Children with the most serious emotional disturbances may exhibit distorted thinking, excessive anxiety, bizarre motor acts, and abnormal mood swings. Some are identified as children who have a severe psychosis or schizophrenia.

Many children who do not have emotional disturbances may display some of these same behaviors at various times during their development. However, when children have an emotional disturbance, these behaviors continue over long periods of time. Their behavior thus signals that they are not coping with their environment or peers.

The educational programs for children with an emotional disturbance need to include attention to providing emotional and behavioral support as well as helping them to master academics; develop social skills; and increase self-awareness, self-control, and self-esteem. A large body of research exists regarding methods of providing students with positive behavioral support (PBS) in the school environment, so that problem behaviors are minimized and positive, appropriate behaviors are fostered. Here are a few important considerations regarding the school setting:

- For a child whose behavior impedes learning (including the learning of others), the team developing the child's individualized education program (IEP) needs to consider, if appropriate, strategies to address that behavior, including positive behavioral interventions, strategies, and supports.

- Students eligible for special education services under the category of emotional disturbance may have IEPs that include psychological or counseling services. These are important related services that are available under law and are to be provided by a qualified social worker, psychologist, guidance counselor, or other qualified personnel.

- Career education (both vocational and academic) is also a major part of secondary education and should be a part of the transition plan included in every adolescent's IEP.

There is growing recognition that families, as well as their children, need support, respite care, intensive case management, and a collaborative, multiagency approach to services. Many communities are working toward providing these wrap-around services. There are a growing number of agencies and organizations actively involved in establishing support services in the community.

Families of children with emotional disturbances may need help in understanding their children's condition and in learning how to work effectively with them. Help is available from psychiatrists, psychologists, or other mental health professionals in public or private mental health settings. Children should be provided services based on their individual needs, and all persons who are involved with these children should be aware of the care they are receiving. It is important to coordinate all services between home, school, and therapeutic community with open communication.[3]

Notes

1. Code of Federal Regulations, Title 34, Section 300.7(c)(4)(i).
2. Code of Federal Regulations, Title 34, Section 300.7(c)(4)(ii).
3. Special thanks to NICHCY (National Dissemination Center for Children with Disabilities) Fact Sheet #5, www.nichcy.org.

CHAPTER NINE

~

Epilepsy

According to the Epilepsy Foundation of America, epilepsy is a physical condition that occurs when there is a sudden, brief change in how the brain works. When brain cells are not working properly, a person's consciousness, movement, or actions may be altered for a short time. These physical changes are called epileptic seizures. Epilepsy is therefore sometimes called a seizure disorder. Epilepsy affects people in all nations and of all races.

Some people can experience a seizure and not have epilepsy. For example, many young children have convulsions from fevers. These febrile convulsions are one type of seizure. Other types of seizures not classified as epilepsy include those caused by an imbalance of body fluids or chemicals or by alcohol or drug withdrawal. A single seizure does not mean that the person has epilepsy.

About 2 million Americans have epilepsy; of the 125,000 new cases that develop each year, up to 50 percent are in children and adolescents.

Although the symptoms listed below are not necessarily indicators of epilepsy, it is wise to consult a doctor if you or a member of your family experiences one or more of them:

- "Blackouts" or periods of confused memory
- Episodes of staring or unexplained periods of unresponsiveness
- Involuntary movement of arms and legs
- "Fainting spells" with incontinence or followed by excessive fatigue
- Odd sounds, distorted perceptions, episodic feelings of fear that cannot be explained

Seizures can be generalized, meaning that all brain cells are involved. One type of generalized seizure consists of a convulsion with a complete loss of consciousness. Another type looks like a brief period of fixed staring.

Seizures are partial when those brain cells not working properly are limited to one part of the brain. Such partial seizures may cause periods of "automatic behavior" and altered consciousness. This is typified by behavior that seems purposeful, such as buttoning or unbuttoning a shirt. Such behavior, however, is unconscious, may be repetitive, and is usually not recalled.

Students with epilepsy or seizure disorders are eligible for special education and related services under the Individuals with Disabilities Education Act (IDEA). Epilepsy is classified as "other health impaired" and an individualized education program (IEP) would be developed to specify appropriate services. Some students may have additional conditions such as learning disabilities along with the seizure disorders.

Seizures may interfere with the child's ability to learn. If the student has the type of seizure characterized by a brief period of fixed staring, he or she may be missing parts of what the teacher is saying. It is important that the teacher observe and document these episodes and report them promptly to parents and to school nurses.

Depending on the type of seizure or how often they occur, some children may need additional assistance to help them keep up with classmates. Assistance can include adaptations in classroom instruction, first aid instruction on seizure management to the student's teachers, and counseling, all of which should be written in the IEP.

It is important that the teachers and school staff are informed about the child's condition, possible effects of medication, and what to do in case a seizure occurs at school. Most parents find that a friendly conversation with the teacher(s) at the beginning of the school year is the best way to handle the situation. Even if a child has seizures that are largely controlled by medication, it is still best to notify the school staff about the condition. School personnel and the family should work together to monitor the effectiveness of medication as well as any side effects. If a child's physical or intellectual skills seem to change, it is important to tell the doctor. There may also be associated hearing or perception problems caused by the brain changes. Written observations of both the family and school staff will be helpful in discussions with the child's doctor.

Children and youth with epilepsy must also deal with the psychological and social aspects of the condition. These include public misperceptions and fear of seizures, uncertain occurrence, loss of self-control during the seizure episode, and compliance with medications. To help children feel more self-confident and accept their epilepsy, the school can assist by providing epilepsy education programs for staff and students, including information on seizure recognition and first aid.

Students can benefit the most when both the family and school are working together. There are many materials available for families and teachers that can aid them in understanding how to work most effectively as a team.[1]

Note

1. Special thanks to NICHCY (National Dissemination Center for Children with Disabilities) Fact Sheet #6, www.nichcy.org.

CHAPTER   TEN

~

Learning Disabilities

Sara's Story

When Sara was in the first grade, her teacher started teaching the students how to read. Sara's parents were really surprised when Sara had a lot of trouble. She was bright and eager, so they thought that reading would come easily to her. It didn't. She couldn't match the letters to their sounds or combine the letters to create words.

Sara's problems continued into second grade. She still wasn't reading, and she was having trouble with writing, too. The school asked Sara's mom for permission to evaluate Sara to find out what was causing her problems. Sara's mom gave permission for the evaluation.

The school conducted an evaluation and learned that Sara has a learning disability. She started getting special help in school right away.

Sara is still getting that special help. She works with a reading specialist and a resource room teacher every day. She's in the fourth grade now, and she's made real progress! She is working hard to bring her reading and writing up to grade level. With help from the school, she'll keep learning and doing well.

Learning Disability Defined

Learning disability is a general term that describes specific kinds of learning problems. A learning disability can cause a person to have trouble learning and using certain skills. The skills most often affected are: reading, writing, listening, speaking, reasoning, and doing math. Learning disabilities (LD) vary from person to person. One person with LD may not have the same kind of learning problems as another person with LD. Sara, in our example above, has trouble with reading and writing. Another person with LD may have problems with understanding math. Still another person may have trouble in each of these areas, as well as with understanding what people are saying.

Researchers think that learning disabilities are caused by differences in how a person's brain works and how it processes information. Children with learning disabilities are not "dumb" or "lazy." In fact, they usually have average or above average intelligence. Their brains just process information differently.

The definition of *learning disability* below comes from the Individuals with Disabilities Education Act (IDEA). The IDEA is the federal law that guides how schools provide special education and related services to children with disabilities. The special help that Sara is receiving is an example of special education.

There is no "cure" for learning disabilities. They are lifelong. However, children with LD can be high achievers and can be taught ways to get around the learning disability. With the right help, children with LD can and do learn successfully.

Our nation's special education law, the Individuals with Disabilities Education Act, defines a specific learning disability as

> a disorder in one or more of the basic psychological processes involved in understanding or in using language, spoken or written, that may manifest itself in an imperfect ability to listen, think, speak, read, write, spell, or do mathematical calculations, including conditions such as perceptual disabilities, brain injury, minimal brain dysfunction, dyslexia, and developmental aphasia.[1]

However, learning disabilities do *not* include "learning problems that are primarily the result of visual, hearing, or motor disabilities, of mental retardation, of emotional disturbance, or of environmental, cultural, or economic disadvantage."[2]

There is no *one* sign that shows a person has a learning disability. Experts look for a noticeable difference between how well a child does in school and how well he or she *could* do, given his or her intelligence or ability. There are also certain clues that may mean a child has a learning disability. Most relate to elementary school tasks, because learning disabilities tend to be identified in elementary school. A child probably won't show all of these signs, or even most of them. However, if a child shows a number of these problems, then parents and the teacher should consider the possibility that the child has a learning disability.

When a child has a learning disability, he or she:

- may have trouble learning the alphabet, rhyming words, or connecting letters to their sounds;
- may make many mistakes when reading aloud, and repeat and pause often;
- may not understand what he or she reads;
- may have real trouble with spelling;
- may have very messy handwriting or hold a pencil awkwardly;
- may struggle to express ideas in writing;
- may learn language late and have a limited vocabulary;
- may have trouble remembering the sounds that letters make or hearing slight differences between words;
- may have trouble understanding jokes, comic strips, and sarcasm;
- may have trouble following directions;
- may mispronounce words or use a wrong word that sounds similar;
- may have trouble organizing what he or she wants to say or not be able to think of the word he or she needs for writing or conversation;
- may not follow the social rules of conversation, such as taking turns, and may stand too close to the listener;
- may confuse math symbols and misread numbers;
- may not be able to retell a story in order (what happened first, second, third); or
- may not know where to begin a task or how to go on from there.

If a child has unexpected problems learning to read, write, listen, speak, or do math, then teachers and parents may want to investigate more. The same is true if the child is struggling to do any one of these skills. The child may need to be evaluated to see if he or she has a learning disability.

Learning disabilities tend to be diagnosed when children reach school age. This is because school focuses on the very things that may be difficult for the child—reading, writing, math, listening, speaking, reasoning. Teachers and parents notice that the child is not learning as expected. The school may ask to evaluate the child to see what is causing the problem. Parents can also ask for their child to be evaluated.

With hard work and the proper help, children with LD can learn more easily and successfully. For school-aged children (including preschoolers), special education and related services are important sources of help. School staff work with the child's parents to develop an individualized education program, or IEP. This document describes the child's unique needs. It also describes the special education services that will be provided to meet those needs. These services are provided at no cost to the child or family.

Supports or changes in the classroom (sometimes called *accommodations*) help most students with LD. Some common accommodations are listed below in "Tips for Teachers." Assistive technology can also help many students work around their learning disabilities. Assistive technology can range from "low-tech" equipment such as tape recorders to "high-tech" tools such as reading machines (which read books aloud) and voice recognition systems (which allow the student to "write" by talking to the computer).

It's important to remember that a child may need help at home as well as in school. The resources listed below will help families and teachers learn more about the many ways to help children with learning disabilities.

Tips for Teachers and Parents

- Learn about LD. The more you know, the more you can help yourself and your child.
- Praise your child when he or she does well. Children with LD are often very good at a variety of things. Find out what your child re-

ally enjoys doing, such as dancing, playing soccer, or working with computers. Give your child plenty of opportunities to pursue his or her strengths and talents.

- Find out the ways your child learns best. Does he or she learn by hands-on practice, looking, or listening? Help your child learn through his or her areas of strength.
- Let your child help with household chores. These can build self-confidence and concrete skills. Keep instructions simple, break down tasks into smaller steps, and reward your child's efforts with praise.
- Make homework a priority. Read more about how to help your child be a success at homework.
- Pay attention to your child's mental health (and your own!). Be open to counseling, which can help your child deal with frustration, feel better about himself or herself, and learn more about social skills.
- Talk to other parents whose children have learning disabilities. Parents can share practical advice and emotional support.
- Meet with school personnel and help develop an educational plan to address your child's needs. Plan what accommodations your child needs, and don't forget to talk about assistive technology!
- Establish a positive working relationship with your child's teacher. Through regular communication, exchange information about your child's progress at home and at school.
- Find out and emphasize what the student's strengths and interests are. Give the student positive feedback and lots of opportunities for practice.
- Review the child's evaluation records to identify where *specifically* the child has trouble.
- Talk to specialists in your school (e.g., special education teacher) about methods for teaching this student. Provide instruction and accommodations to address the student's special needs. Examples include:
  - breaking tasks into smaller steps, and giving directions verbally and in writing;
  - giving the student more time to finish schoolwork or take tests;

o letting the student with reading problems use textbooks-on-tape (available through Recording for the Blind and Dyslexic; see "Organizations" at the back of this book);

o letting the student with listening difficulties borrow notes from a classmate or use a tape recorder; and

o letting the student with writing difficulties use a computer with specialized software that spell checks, grammar checks, or recognizes speech.

• Learn about the different testing modifications that can really help a student with LD show what he or she has learned.

• Teach organizational skills, study skills, and learning strategies. These help all students but are particularly helpful to those with LD.

• Work together to create an educational plan tailored to meet the student's needs. Keep communication lines open concerning the child's progress at home and school.[3]

Notes

1. Individuals with Disabilities Education Act (Pub. L. No. 108-446, 118 Stat. 2647).

2. 34 Code of Federal Regulations §300.7(c)(10).

3. Special thanks to NICHCY (National Dissemination Center for Children with Disabilities) Fact Sheet #7, www.nichcy.org.

CHAPTER ELEVEN

~

Traumatic Brain Injury

Susan's Story

Susan was seven years old when she was hit by a car while riding her bike. She broke her arm and leg. She also hit her head very hard. The doctors say she sustained a traumatic brain injury. When she came home from the hospital, she needed lots of help, but now she looks fine.

In fact, that's part of the problem, especially at school. Her friends and teachers think her brain has healed because her broken bones have. But there are changes in Susan that are hard to understand. It takes Susan longer to do things. She has trouble remembering things. She can't always find the words she wants to use. Reading is hard for her now. It's going to take time before people really understand the changes they see in her.

Traumatic Brain Injury Defined

Our nation's special education law, the Individuals with Disabilities Education Act (IDEA) defines *traumatic brain injury* as

an acquired injury to the brain caused by an external physical force, resulting in total or partial functional disability or psychosocial impairment, or both, that adversely affects a child's educational performance. The term applies to open or closed head injuries resulting in impairments in one or more areas, such as cognition; language; memory; attention; reasoning; abstract thinking; judgment; problem-solving; sensory, perceptual, and motor abilities; psycho-social behavior; physical functions; information processing; and speech. The term does not apply to brain injuries that are congenital or degenerative, or to brain injuries induced by birth trauma.[1]

A traumatic brain injury (TBI) is an injury to the brain caused by the head being hit by something or shaken violently. This injury can change how the person acts, moves, and thinks. A traumatic brain injury can also change how a student learns and acts in school. The term TBI is used for head injuries that can cause changes in one or more areas, such as:

- thinking and reasoning,
- understanding words,
- remembering things,
- paying attention,
- solving problems,
- thinking abstractly,
- talking,
- behaving,
- walking and other physical activities,
- seeing and/or hearing, and
- learning.

The term TBI is not used for a person who is born with a brain injury. It also is not used for brain injuries that happen during birth.

The signs of brain injury can be very different depending on where the brain is injured and how severely. Children with TBI may have one or more difficulties, including:

- *Physical disabilities:* Individuals with TBI may have problems speaking, seeing, hearing, and using their other senses. They may have headaches and feel tired a lot. They may also have trouble with skills such as writing or drawing. Their muscles may suddenly contract or tighten (this is called spasticity). They may also have seizures. Their balance and walking may also be affected. They may be partly or completely paralyzed on one side of the body, or both sides.

- *Difficulties with thinking*: Because the brain has been injured, it is common that the person's ability to use the brain changes. For example, children with TBI may have trouble with short-term memory (being able to remember something from one minute to the next, like what the teacher just said). They may also have trouble with their long-term memory (being able to remember information from a while ago, like facts learned last month). People with TBI may have trouble concentrating and only be able to focus their attention for a short time. They may think slowly. They may have trouble talking and listening to others. They may also have difficulty with reading and writing, planning, understanding the order in which events happen (called sequencing), and judgment.

- *Social, behavioral, or emotional problems*: These difficulties may include sudden changes in mood, anxiety, and depression. Children with TBI may have trouble relating to others. They may be restless and may laugh or cry a lot. They may not have much motivation or much control over their emotions.

A child with TBI may not have all of the above difficulties. Brain injuries can range from mild to severe, and so can the changes that result from the injury. This means that it's hard to predict how an individual will recover from the injury. Early and ongoing help can make a big difference in how the child recovers. This help can include physical or occupational therapy, counseling, and special education.

It's also important to know that, as the child grows and develops, parents and teachers may notice new problems. This is because, as students grow, they are expected to use their brain in new and different ways. The damage to the brain from the earlier injury can make it hard for the student to learn new skills that come with getting older. Sometimes parents and educators may not even realize that the student's difficulty comes from the earlier injury.

Although TBI is very common, many medical and education professionals may not realize that some difficulties can be caused by a childhood brain injury. Often, students with TBI are thought to have a learning disability, emotional disturbance, or mental retardation. As a result, they don't receive the type of educational help and support they really need.

When children with TBI return to school, their educational and emotional needs are often very different than before the injury. Their disability has happened suddenly and traumatically. They can often remember how they were before the brain injury. This can bring on many emotional and social changes. The child's family, friends, and teachers also recall what the child was like before the injury. These other people in the child's life may have trouble changing or adjusting their expectations of the child.

Therefore, it is extremely important to plan carefully for the child's return to school. Parents will want to find out ahead of time about special education services at the school. This information is usually available from the school's principal or special education teacher. The school will need to evaluate the child thoroughly. This evaluation will let the school and parents know what the student's educational needs are. The school and parents will then develop an individualized education program (IEP) that addresses those educational needs.

It's important to remember that the IEP is a flexible plan. It can be changed as the parents, the school, and the student learn more about what the student needs at school.

Tips for Parents and Teachers

- Learn about TBI. The more you know, the more you can help yourself and your child.
- Work with the medical team to understand your child's injury and treatment plan. Don't be shy about asking questions. Tell them what you know or think. Make suggestions.
- Keep track of your child's treatment. A three-ring binder or a box can help you store this history. As your child recovers, you may meet with many doctors, nurses, and others. Write down what they say. Put any paperwork they give you in the notebook or throw it in the box. You can't remember all this! Also, if you need to share any of this paperwork with someone else, make a copy. Don't give away your original!

- Talk to other parents whose children have TBI. There are parent groups all over the United States. Parents can share practical advice and emotional support.
- If your child was in school before the injury, plan for his or her return to school. Get in touch with the school. Ask the principal about special education services. Have the medical team share information with the school.
- When your child returns to school, ask the school to test your child as soon as possible to identify his or her special education needs. Meet with the school and help develop an IEP.
- Keep in touch with your child's teacher. Tell the teacher about how your child is doing at home. Ask how your child is doing in school.
- Give the student more time to finish schoolwork and tests.
- Give directions one step at a time. For tasks with many steps, it helps to give the student written directions.
- Show the student how to perform new tasks. Give examples to go with new ideas and concepts.
- Have consistent routines. This helps the child know what to expect. If the routine is going to change, let the student know ahead of time.
- Check to make sure that the child has actually learned the new skill. Give the student lots of opportunities to practice the new skill.
- Show the student how to use an assignment book and a daily schedule. This helps the student get organized.
- Realize that the student may get tired quickly. Let the student rest as needed.
- Reduce distractions.
- Share information about how the student is doing at home and at school.[2]

Notes

1. 34 Code of Federal Regulations §300.7(c)(12).
2. Special thanks to NICHCY (National Dissemination Center for Children with Disabilities) Fact Sheet #18, www.nichcy.org.

CHAPTER TWELVE

~

Visual Impairments

The terms "partially sighted," "low vision," "legally blind," and "totally blind" are used in the educational context to describe students with visual impairments. They are defined as follows:

1. "Partially sighted" indicates some type of visual problem has resulted in a need for special education.
2. "Low vision" generally refers to a severe visual impairment, not necessarily limited to distance vision. Low vision applies to all individuals with sight who are unable to read the newspaper at a normal viewing distance, even with the aid of eyeglasses or contact lenses. They use a combination of vision and other senses to learn, although they may require adaptations in lighting or the size of print, and, sometimes, Braille.
3. "Legally blind" indicates that a person has less than 20/200 vision in the better eye or a very limited field of vision (20 degrees at its widest point).
4. Totally blind students learn via Braille or other nonvisual media.

Visual impairment is the consequence of a functional loss of vision, rather than the eye disorder itself. Eye disorders that can lead to visual impairments can include retinal degeneration, albinism, cataracts, glaucoma, muscular problems that result in visual disturbances, corneal disorders, diabetic retinopathy, congenital disorders, and infection.

The rate at which visual impairments occur in individuals under the age of eighteen is 12.2 per 1,000. Severe visual impairments (legally or totally blind) occur at a rate of .06 per 1,000.

The effect of visual problems on a child's development depends on the severity, type of loss, age at which the condition appears, and overall functioning level of the child. Many children who have multiple disabilities may also have visual impairments resulting in motor, cognitive, and/or social developmental delays.

A young child with visual impairments has little reason to explore interesting objects in the environment and, thus, may miss opportunities to have experiences and to learn. This lack of exploration may continue until learning becomes motivating or until intervention begins.

Because the child cannot see parents or peers, he or she may be unable to imitate social behavior or understand nonverbal cues. Visual handicaps can create obstacles to a growing child's independence.

Children with visual impairments should be assessed early to benefit from early intervention programs, when applicable. Technology in the form of computers and low-vision optical and video aids enable many partially sighted, low-vision, and blind children to participate in regular class activities. Large-print materials, books on tape, and Braille books are available.

Students with visual impairments may need additional help with special equipment and modifications in the regular curriculum to emphasize listening skills, communication, orientation and mobility, vocation/career options, and daily living skills. Students with low vision or those who are legally blind may need help in using their residual vision more efficiently and in working with special aids and materials. Students who have visual impairments combined with other types of disabilities have a greater need for an interdisciplinary approach and may require greater emphasis on self-care and daily living skills.[1]

Note

1. Special thanks to NICHCY (National Dissemination Center for Children with Disabilities) Fact Sheet #13, www.nichcy.org.

~

CHAPTER THIRTEEN

Four Questions and Answers

Question from a Parent of a
Twice-Exceptional Student

Q: My husband has attended your sessions at the CJE in Baltimore. I have a twice-exceptional child—very high IQ, a complete inability to read social cues, and great social awkwardness.

His school is destroying him. I have tried to work with the teachers and the school district. They have told me to "not phone or e-mail, as these will not be responded to—that I am to leave my child to make decisions on his own." I have teachers who refuse to have contact with me. I am confident that they are retaliating against my son because of my advocating on his behalf. The school's stance is since he is not failing academically, then "he is fine."

My son has had thoughts of suicide at the age of eight. The school is aware of this, but continues to use him as a punching bag.

I feel as though I have exhausted my efforts—I have been to G/T advocates, special education advocates, the deputy superintendent of our county, his psychologist, and so on. All the literature I have read has stressed, "your child will succeed as well as his teachers want him to succeed." His teachers just want him to go away, and the principal is in complete support of this. The teachers have told me, "If an activity does not improve test scores, then we cannot justify it to the school district."

I am at a complete loss. I am trying to find the balance of between how far do you push and when to back off.

I am continually told that my son does not have "disabilities" as he is so intelligent. Yet, all the tests and experts with whom I speak refer to my son as "special needs." However, the school refuses to classify him as "special needs" as he is in the G/T program (which . . . the teachers are telling me that he is "falling down").

Any help/assistance/insight you can provide would be greatly appreciated. The school system is destroying my son and literally killing me.

A: I am so very sad to read this. Please know I understand your frustration and hope my suggestions can help you sort your problems out.

I believe there are a couple of issues at work here.

Since NCLB has been enacted, teachers and school districts have become even more focused on raising student test scores to validate funding and show adequate progress of the lower-achieving students. "Teaching to the tests" has become a chronic condition in many education arenas. I see this every semester with my graduate students. I continue to be stunned when they repeatedly tell me that their administrators are constantly pressuring them to "teach to the tests" and get the students' scores up! I keep suggesting that if the teachers focused on teaching all students to think, taking all children to the synthesis and evaluation levels, district scores would not only rise, but become exemplary! I am dismayed by the lack of understanding of the importance of teaching children to think, create, and evaluate! I am reminded of the proverb, "You can give a starving man a fish to eat, but if you don't teach him how to fish, he'll continue to starve."

I suspect focusing on teaching to the tests is why your son's teachers are saying, "If an activity does not improve test scores, then we cannot justify doing it to the school district."

I'm not agreeing with this philosophy, but I am trying to explain to you why this could be happening.

Also, it sounds like you and the school district are at odds, especially when you say your son's teachers have said, "not to phone or e-mail," as you will not receive a response. This sounds pretty drastic on the school district's side! As a former teacher in the public schools for over thirty years, I can honestly say I had my share of verbal attacks, one or two that were ruthless. I have always considered myself an ongoing advocate for gifted children, their parents, and all children. To be attacked came as a shock to me.

No one wants to be blindsided or treated disrespectfully. In frustration, could you have approached your son's teacher(s) in anger?

For any future meetings or discussions, it would be advantageous to have an advocate with you who can calmly and directly present your concerns to your son's educators and all other concerned adults. Your advocate could be the school counselor or psychologist, G/T coordinator, your son's pediatrician, his private psychologist, or a specialist in twice-exceptional children.

May I assume you have documentation from the experts and test results you mentioned indicating your son is a special-needs child?

IDEA—the Individuals with Disabilities Education Act—will be your best ally now. As our nation's special education law, IDEA guides how states provide early intervention and special education services to children and youth with disabilities.

I also encourage you to access the website of NICHCY Connections at www.NICHCY.org/idea.htm for invaluable information, leads, suggestions, and help, or contact NICHCY @1-800-695-0258, NICHCY@aed .org or NICHCY.org.

NICHCY will be your guidebook for every future step of your way in the education system. Please remember, you can also always contact me by e-mail at szulgit2@aol.com.

Please keep me informed.

Question from a Teacher

Q: I have a student who is gifted and probably ADHD . . . impulsive, inappropriate behaviors, currently taking medication to help her function. How can I redirect her, help keep her focused and interested in class?

A: One of the helpful strategies I believe we often overlook in education is including the student in a discussion of what her interfering behaviors are and talking about strategies for better student success. If there is a mutual trust among the teacher, student, parent, and caseworker, the child is often more willing to try suggested strategies, especially if she has been included in the strategy planning sessions. It is so easy to get into a disciplinary mode rather than a behavior modification role as the teacher or parent. I know this is easier said than done, but hopefully a good reminder for all of us.

Question from a 2E Student

Q: I am a thirteen-year-old student identified as twice-exceptional in an affluent suburban school district. Because my parents have been very persistent in advocating for my best education placement, I have been identified, labeled, and treated as a special education student, receiving help in a resource room as twice-exceptional. I can't stand it. First, I don't like being singled out as a child with special needs. Second, the teacher seems to constantly focus on my weaknesses rather than letting me accelerate in math and writing, which are my strengths. I've talked to my parents about my feelings many times, but they believe I'm better off with special services. What do you think? I'm at the point where I don't even want to go to school anymore.

A: This is a classic good news/bad news situation. The good news is you have parents who proactively seek out the services due you within the guidelines of your school district as a twice-exceptional student. Further good news is your school district acknowledges the special education category of 2E and tries to provide helpful classroom assistance. Just as I've seen many gifted programs do more harm than good by piling on homework at grade level instruction or even accelerated, it is not uncommon in 2E classrooms or resource situations to focus on the remediation of students' weaknesses in excess rather than working with their gifted intellectual strengths. I truly understand your frustrations. I would like to suggest the following options to you:

- As I mentioned in an earlier Q/A, no one likes to be blindsided, so I would like you to first talk with your teacher about possible acceleration activities, rather than focusing on your disability. While we work together to gain a greater balance in twice-exceptional education, a child such as yourself may still bear the brunt of lopsided services. If your teacher is not receptive, please have the courage to talk to your school's gifted coordinator. If there isn't a person in your specific school, there will be one for the district. Call, write, or e-mail in confidence explaining your situation. Be positive and supportive. Many times when parents or students are really frustrated, they can be a bit antagonistic rather than having a proactive attitude of working together with the education personnel and system to solve the problem.

- It sounds like you've tried to explain your feelings to your parents. I'm sure they've worked very diligently to get you the special education services they think you should have and don't want to upset the apple cart. I can understand where they're coming from. Yet, it's up to you to help them work with you to get a more positive emotional and intellectual schooling for you. Try writing them a letter if they haven't seemed to listen in the past. Again, be positive and proactive and talk about the things that you want their help with toward your happiness and success. It's worth a try.

- Find out who your state coordinator for gifted is and contact her, explaining your situation. In every state we know there is room for improvement in 2E services. Yours could be the test case for future and more appropriate education for twice-exceptional students.

- E-mail me at szulgit2@aol.com and we can correspond discussing day-to-day issues that we can try and solve step-by-step. Please stay in touch. I will try and help you, your parents, and teacher as best I can.

Question from a Language Arts Supervisor

Q: In a forty-five-minute class, what specific activities can I offer teachers to provide for their gifted student(s) to keep them stimulated and learning?

A: Project Success Enrichment (PSE), a nationally recognized, exemplary language arts and writing program, is very powerful and student oriented. Students love it, and their writing skills improve overnight. It is the best I have seen on the market throughout my entire career! Once you investigate PSE, you'll see this exemplary program has everything 6+1 Traits and other popular writing programs have, plus phenomenal creativity tied into integrative and spell-binding lessons! I can't praise this program enough. Getting your entire staff of teachers trained in PSE would be the best gift you could give them and all their students, including 2E! Additional information is available from the PSE website: www.projse.com or by e-mailing its founder/director Carolyn Bronson at Bronson@methownet.com.

CHAPTER FOURTEEN

~

Advocacy for the Twice-Exceptional

Self

Many times a low self-esteem or inability with social communications of the twice-exceptional child can make self-advocacy very difficult. Even so, you and your parents should and must be your number one and number two advocates. To begin, you need to understand your disability—how it interferes with the expression of your intelligence, patterns of behavior, and successful academic and social experiences. Once your school psychologist or private practitioner has correctly diagnosed your learning disability, seek out the research on it, finding as much information and as many helpful resources as you can. You'll gain valuable information on how to compensate for and redirect your abilities. With understanding and practice, your education and life will become less stressful and more positive, and you'll definitely become more proactive! You'll also be learning what your education rights are, which can help you legally if you and your parents run into resistance.

Parent

Throughout my career as an educator advocating for the rights of gifted and all children, the biggest mistake I've seen parent advocates make is the expression of their frustrations through anger and ferocity toward teachers, administrators, and their local school districts. Before you lose a proper and healthy perspective, please align yourself with an advocate in your child's school, preferably one who is knowledgeable in twice-exceptional, gifted children, gifted education, and learning disabilities. Local hospital and mental health clinics should be able to provide you with a list of qualified health care professionals. You want to be valued as working with the system, rather than attacking it. Another valuable resource for finding a psychologist trained and supportive of gifted children and their education can be accessed on the Internet at www .sengifted.org under the heading of "Selecting a Mental Health Professional for Your Gifted Child." I have also included a listing of websites and advocacy groups in the back of the book. Once you have stabilized your 2E child's support systems, you might even consider forming your own parent advocacy group to help those who follow you in the system. Always remember, you can contact me at szulgit2@aol.com whenever you need additional help or advice. I will be glad to respond.

While advocates for twice-exceptional children certainly have their own road less traveled to walk in support of the intellectually gifted/learning disabled, I feel it worthwhile to include James Delisle's "Top Ten Statements That Should Never Again Be Made by Advocates of Gifted Children" as a reminder to all of us who want the best for all our students and to bring a smile or two if we become too intent on our missions.

10. Only gifted students can really do in-depth, independent projects.

I've known identified gifted students who couldn't care less about long-term investigations of "real problems" and non-identified students who shine when given the chance to explore an interest in depth. Let's stop kidding ourselves that only identified gifted students have the wherewithal to complete complex assignments and instead realize the obvious: Doing well depends as much on attitude as it does on aptitude.

9. Twenty percent of all high school dropouts are gifted.

This myth has been perpetuated for years and, for the life of me, I can't determine where this figure comes from. The only rational voice on this issue was presented by David Irvine in an *Educational Leadership* article, "What Research Doesn't Show About Gifted Dropouts" (1987). He determined numerically that, if this 20 percent figure were accurate, it would mean that every gifted student in our nation drops out of high school. I'm all for getting people to support gifted education, but citing false data is something I cannot support.

8. Gifted students are more prone to depression and suicide than nongifted students.

Related to the myth about dropouts, this "scare tactic" has been cited for years even though there is no research evidence to back it up. Having studied both of these issues extensively, I can assert unequivocally that, although suicide and depression among gifted students are serious concerns, their prevalence is no more frequent than it is for nongifted adolescents. If we are to advocate for mental health education for teenagers and children, let's do so for all children.

7. Today's gifted students are tomorrow's leaders who will solve the world's problems.

I'm not sure who should be most irate about this assertion—the gifted students who seem obligated to save their world or the "nongifted" students who apparently are bystanders to global change. Either way, the statement is both unfair and unfounded. We can no more predict that today's gifted children will remedy their world as we can assert that today's politicians and "change agents" were all involved in gifted programs when they were youngsters. When will we realize that history and social improvement are not as predictable as we sometimes make them out to be.

6. Cooperative learning should not be used with gifted students—they're just made into "little teachers."

I will be the first to admit that many practices that occur under the guise of "cooperative learning" are detrimental to gifted students. However, the idea of cooperative learning, in which students work as teams to draw out each others' academic strengths and interests, should not be considered bad. In fact, when done well and appropriately, I can think of no better way than cooperative learning to integrate gifted education principles into the repertoire of skills useful for classroom teachers. Don't fault a good concept because it is being implemented poorly. Instead, change the method of operation so that it becomes advantageous for all its participants.

5. Underachievement happens when children aren't challenged in school.

Granted there is some connection between academic rigor and one's desire to achieve at a high level. Still, the topic of underachievement is so complex and it involves so much more than purely academic conditions (e.g., self-concept, family relations, school climate) that to blame underachievement on a lack of intellectual rigor is to oversimplify a very complex problem. Children who underachieve in school must be looked at individually, not as a conglomerate, intact group if positive changes are to occur in their lives.

4. We need to identify children who are truly gifted.

First of all, "truly" or otherwise, many gifted children identify themselves through their behaviors, vocabularies, emotions or actions. To state that we seek to identify only "truly" gifted children implies that somewhere out there exists a cluster of capable children who can be found as long as we use the right tests or performance scales. I prefer a simpler mode: Let's look at what children need in school and other places and give them the opportunities they need to enhance their individual talents. Then, identifying giftedness becomes less of an issue while providing appropriate services becomes paramount in importance.

3. Classroom teachers cannot possibly meet the needs of gifted children in a regular classroom.

When this falsehood is stated, the speaker usually exhibits an aura of compassion: "Oh, pity the poor classroom teacher. He or she has *so* many children, so many requirements, *so* little time." Well, sorry. Rather than take away one of the few remnants of respect that classroom teachers still hold—that is, that they know how to plan instruction based on the needs of students—I'd rather assume they are trying the best they know how and that it is my role, as a gifted education specialist, to help them become even better than they already are.

2. Gifted students are bored in regular classrooms.

Boring is one of those buzzwords that sends teachers into spasms. How often a child has told me that he or she is bored in school, and how often I followed this assertion with a classroom observation in which said "bored" student was smiling and participating to the max. Before we ascribe as strong an adjective as *boring* to a teacher or classroom, let us first determine what this amorphous word really means.

1. Without a gifted program, this student will never reach full potential.

First of all, who among us has reached his or her "full potential"? And, if you have, how do you know that you did? *Potential* is perhaps the most misused word in our gifted lexicon as it implies that someone other than ourselves knows the limits of what we can accomplish. To add an even bigger measure of insult to this assertion, we sometimes state that the only way to reach one's potential is to be in a gifted program. Forget parents and excellent classroom teachers and personal aspirations—it's the gifted program that makes us reach for the stars. Sorry . . . that's probably not entirely true.[1]

Note

1. Excerpted from James R. Delisle, *Barefoot Irreverence: A Guide to Critical Issues in Gifted Child Education* (Austin, TX: Prufrock Press, Inc., 2002), 213–15. Reprinted by permission of the publisher.

CHAPTER FIFTEEN

~

Twice-Exceptional Children
Speak to Us

During the process of researching and writing this book, I interviewed several fifth and sixth graders who had been identified as 2E in their school settings. I asked the following two questions:

1. What was the one factor in school that kept them from succeeding in the past?
2. What was working best for them now in an inclusion classroom or resource room?

Following are their overwhelmingly similar answers.

Q1. What was the one factor in school that had kept the 2E child from succeeding in the past?

- I couldn't do the work and no one cared. They just kept trying to make me do it the same way. Jeff, age 11.
- I liked math but had to do the same work as everyone else in class. I would have liked to do more challenging and different math assignments. Cara, age 12.
- I couldn't transfer my thoughts on to paper well. Writing wasn't one of my strengths, yet I still was made to write in my journal everyday. Steve, age 12.

Q2. What was helping the 2E child succeed most now in an inclusion classroom or resource room?

- I can use the computer to type my writing assignments. It helps me be more neat and organized. Jo Ellen, age 12.
- I don't have to do things the same way as everyone else. I can draw my answers. Brad, age 11.
- I can tape record my spelling sentences and vocabulary words. It is so much easier for me. Jack, age 12.
- My teacher understands I can't do things like everyone else and doesn't make me. She helps me find other ways to get my work done. Shelly, age 11.
- Nothing has changed. I still can't succeed. Judy, age 11.

A Good Teacher Through the Eyes of a Gifted Child

By E'Shantee R. Proctor

Acknowledges my uniqueness.
Grants me the opportunities to creatively problem solve.
Opposed to the notion that I must be globally gifted.
Offers enriching opportunities and chances for real-life experiences.
Develops ways for me to learn at my level and pace.
Truly dedicated to my classmates and me.
Eases the tensions with a warm, loving, learning environment.
Appropriately differentiates the curriculum.
Convinced that I don't need to be separated from my peers.
Helps me reach the synthesis level of thinking.
Encourages me to be my best.
Realizes what works for me can work for all of my classmates.

APPENDIX

~

A Sample Individualized Education Program and 504 Plan

A Sample Individualized Education Program

If your twice-exceptional child is eligible for special education services in your school district, you will work along with the Special Education Committee to develop an education plan to meet your child's unique needs. While districts may vary slightly, an individualized education program (IEP) should include the following:

- Your child's name and his disability.
- Your child's current abilities, needs, and evaluation results.
- Annual goals and objectives for your child to meet.
- Special equipment your child may need in school.
- Description of what services, amount of time they will be provided, or special education program your child will receive.
- How your child will take tests, such as longer time periods.
- Program modifications for your child.
- What supports your child's teacher(s) will have to help implement your child's IEP.
- When you will receive progress reports and how.
- Ensuring the least-restrictive environment, recommendations for where your child's services will be provided.

Once an IEP is developed, your Board of Education is responsible for arranging appropriate services and programs to begin for your child, usually within 30 to 60 days and dependent on the specific circumstances of your case.

Quite honestly, even if your 2E child did not qualify for special education placement in your district, I think these IEP guidelines would be helpful to you and the teacher(s) primarily responsible for his appropriate and successful education!

A Sample 504 Plan

Table 1. Section 504 Student Accommodation Plan Pre-Conference

Student:	Meeting Date:
Student Number:	DOB:
Grade:	Building:
Case Manager:	School Year:
Parent/Guardian's Information:	
Parent/Guardian:	Relationship:
Street:	
City:	Zip:
Telephone:	County of Residence:
Dominant Language of Parent/Guardian:	Interpreter Needed:
Parent/Guardian:	Relationship:
Street:	
City:	Zip:
Telephone:	County of Residence:
Dominant Language of Parent/Guardian:	Interpreter Needed:

Part I: Justification for Services

A. There is a physical or mental impairment, which substantially limits one or more major life activity(ies). Some examples of possible 504 disabilities include: allergies, arthritis, attention deficit, diabetes, heart disease, physical disabilities, etc. (disabling condition)

B. Major Life Activity Affected:

C. Briefly document the basis for determining the disability:

Part II: Necessary Accommodations
  A. Educational Impact of Disability:

  B. Necessary Accommodations:

Test Modifications
The following Test Accommodations will be used consistently in the student's educational program, including the administration of district-wide assessments, except as prohibited by SED in the administration of state assessments.

Special Education Safety Net

504 Service

Part III: Significant Medical Information

Part IV. Academic History (Scores/Dates)
- Speech/Language Evaluation:
- Psychological Evaluation:
- Reading:
- Writing:

- Math:

- NYS Assessments:

Meeting Participants:

~

Websites

2e (Twice-Exceptional) Newsletter: www.2enewsletter.com
All Kinds of Minds: www.allkindsofminds.org
A Nation Deceived: http://nationdeceived.org
Association for the Education of Gifted Underachieving Students (AEGUS): www.autism-society.org
Barbara Kirby and Asperger's Syndrome: www.udel.edu/bkirby/ asperger/aswhatisit.html
Center for Talented Youth, Johns Hopkins University: www.jhu.edu/ ~gifted.
Children and Adults with Attention Deficit/Hyperactivity Disorder: www.chadd.org
Council for Exceptional Children: www.cec.sped.org
Davidson Institute for Talent Development: http://ditd.org
Dyscalculia (math learning disability): www.dyscalculia.org
Educational Research and Information Center (ERIC): www.ericec .org
Gifted Development Center: www.gifteddevelopment.com
GT World: www.gtworld.org
Hoagies' Gifted Education: www.hoagiesgifted.org
International Dyslexia Society: http://interdys.org

LD Online: www.ldonline.org

Learning Disabilities Association of America: www.ldanatl.org

National Association for Gifted Children: www.nagc.org

National Center for Learning Disabilities: www.ncld.org

National Dissemination Center for Children with Disabilities: www
.nichcy.org

NLD on the Web: www.nldontheweb.org

Nonverbal Learning Disorders Association: www.nlda.org

Parent Encouragement Program: www.parentencouragement.org

Schwab Learning: www.SchwabLearning.org

Smart Kids with Learning Disabilities: www.smartkidswithld.org

The Gifted with Learning Differences Educational Network: www
.gtldnetwork.org

Uniquely Gifted: www.uniquelygifted.org

Wrightslaw Libraries: www.wrightslaw.com

Yale Child Study Center: www.info.med.yale.edu/chldstdy/autism
.html

~

Organizations

Alexander Graham Bell Association for the Deaf and Hard of Hearing
3417 Volta Place, NW
Washington, DC 20007
202.337.5220 (V); 202.337.5221 (TTY)
E-mail: info@agbell.org
Web: www.agbell.org

American Academy of Child and Adolescent Psychiatry
Public Information Office
3615 Wisconsin Avenue, NW
Washington, DC 20016-3007
202.966.7300
Web: www.aacap.org

American Council of the Blind
1155 15th Street, NW, Suite 1004
Washington, DC 20005
202.467.5081; 800.424.8666
E-mail: info@acb.org
Web: www.acb.org

American Foundation for the Blind
    11 Penn Plaza, Suite 300
    New York, NY 10001
    800.232.5463 (Hotline)
    For publications, call: 800.232.3044
    E-mail: afbinfo@afb.net
    Web: www.afb.org

American Society for Deaf Children
    P.O. Box 3355
    Gettysburg, PA 17325
    800.942.2732 (V/TTY); 717.334.7922 (V/TTY)
    E-mail: ASDC1@aol.com
    Web: www.deafchildren.org

American Speech-Language Hearing Association
    10801 Rockville Pike
    Rockville, MD 20852
    301.897.5700 (V/TTY); 800.638.8255 (V/TTY)
    Web: www.asha.org

The Arc of the United States (formerly the Association for Retarded Citizens of the United States)
    1010 Wayne Avenue, Suite 650
    Silver Spring, MD 20910
    301.565.3842
    E-mail: info@thearc.org
    Web: www.thearc.org

Autism Information Center
    Centers for Disease Control and Prevention
    404-639-3534
    800-311-3435
    Web: www.cdc.gov/ncbddd/dd/ddautism.htm

Autism Society of America
    301-657-0881
    800-328-8476
    Web: www.autism-society.org

Autism Treatment Network
503-783-2710
Web: www.autismtreatmentnetwork.org

Blind Children's Center
4120 Marathon Street
Los Angeles, CA 90029-0159
323.664.2153; 800.222.3566
E-mail: info@blindchildrenscenter.org
Web: www.blindchildrenscenter.org

Brain Injury Association (formerly the National Head Injury Foundation)
8201 Greensboro Drive, Suite 611
McLean, VA 22102
703.761.0750; 800.444.6443 (Family Helpline)
E-mail: FamilyHelpline@biausa.org
Web site: www.biausa.org

Center on Positive Behavioral Interventions and Supports
5262 University of Oregon
Eugene, OR 97403-5262
541.346.2505
E-mail: pbis@oregon.uregon.edu
Web: www.pbis.org

CH.A.D.D. (Children and Adults with Attention-Deficit/Hyperactivity Disorder)
8181 Professional Place, Suite 201
Landover, MD 20785
301-306-7070
800-233-4050
E-mail: national@chadd.org
Web: www.chadd.org

Cure Autism Now
323-549-0500
888-828-8476
Web: www.cureautismnow.org

Division for Learning Disabilities (DLD)
The Council for Exceptional Children (CEC)
1110 North Glebe Road, Suite 300
Arlington, VA 22201-5704
703.620.3660
E-mail: cec@cec.sped.org
Web: www.dldcec.org

Easter Seals—National Office
230 West Monroe Street, Suite 1800
Chicago, IL 60606-4802
800.221.6827 (V)
312.726.6200 (V)
312.726.4258 (TTY)
Web: www.easter-seals.org

Emergency Medical Services for Children—National Resource Center
111 Michigan Avenue NW
Washington, DC 20010
202.884.4927
E-mail: information@emscnrc.com
Web: www.ems-c.org/

Epilepsy Foundation—National Office
4351 Garden City Drive
Landover, MD 20785-7223
301.459.3700; 800.332.1000 (Toll Free)
301.577.0100 for publications
Web: www.epilepsyfoundation.org

ERIC Clearing House on Disabilities and Gifted Education Council for Exceptional Children
1920 Association Drive
Reston, VA 22091-1589
Web: www.cec.sped.org/ericec

Family Caregiver Alliance
    180 Montgomery Street, Suite 1100
    San Francisco, CA 94104
    415.434.3388; 800.445.8106
    E-mail: info@caregiver.org
    Web: www.caregiver.org

Family Voices
    2340 Alamo SE, Suite 102
    Albuquerque, NM 87106
    505.872.4774; 888.835.5669
    E-mail: kidshealth@familyvoices.org
    Web: www.familyvoices.org

Federation of Families for Children's Mental Health
    1101 King Street, Suite 420
    Alexandria, VA 22314
    703.684.7710
    E-mail: ffcmh@ffcmh.org
    Web: www.ffcmh.org

The Foundation Fighting Blindness
    (formerly the National Retinitis Pigmentosa Foundation)
    11435 Cronhill Drive
    Owings Mills, MD 21117-2220
    888.394.3937; 800.683.5551 (TTY)
    410.568.0150; 410.363.7139 (TTY)
    E-mail: info@blindness.org
    Web: www.blindness.org

Head Injury Hotline
    212 Pioneer Building
    Seattle, WA 98104-2221
    206.621.8558
    E-mail: brain@headinjury.com
    Web: www.headinjury.com

Indiana Resource Center for Autism
Indiana Institute on Disability & Community
812-855-6508
812-855-9396 (TTY)
Web: www.iidc.indiana.edu/irca

International Dyslexia Association (formerly the Orton Dyslexia Society)
Chester Building, Suite 382
8600 LaSalle Road
Baltimore, MD 21286-2044
800.222.3123; 410.296.0232
E-mail: info@interdys.org
Web: www.interdys.org

Laurent Clerc National Deaf Education Center
KDES PAS-6, Gallaudet University
800 Florida Avenue N.E.
Washington, DC 20002-3695
202.651.5051 (V/TTY)
E-mail: Clearinghouse.InfoToGo@gallaudet.edu
Web: http://clerccenter.gallaudet.edu/InfoToGo/index.html

Learning Disabilities Association of America (LDA)
4156 Library Road
Pittsburgh, PA 15234-1349
412.341.1515
E-mail: info@ldaamerica.org
Web: www.ldaamerica.org

LDOnline
MAAP Services for Autism & Asperger Syndrome
219.662.1311
Web: www.asperger.org
Web: www.ldonline.org

National Alliance for the Mentally Ill (NAMI)
Colonial Place Three
2107 Wilson Boulevard, Suite 300
Arlington, VA 22203-3754
703.524.7600; 703.516.7227 (TTY)
800.950.6264
Web: www.nami.org

National Alliance for Autism Research
888-777-6227
Web: www.naar.org/

National Association for Parents of the Visually Impaired, Inc.
P.O. Box 317
Watertown, MA 02472-0317
617.972.7441; 800.562.6265
E-mail: napvi@perkins.org
Web: www.napvi.org

National Association for Visually Handicapped
22 West 21st Street, 6th Floor
New York, NY 10010
212.889.3141
E-mail: staff@navh.org
Web: www.navh.org

National Attention Deficit Disorder Association
1788 Second Street, Suite 200
Highland Park, IL 60035
847.432.2332
E-mail: mail@add.org
Web: www.add.org

National Braille Association, Inc. (NBA)
3 Townline Circle
Rochester, NY 14623-2513
585.427.8260

E-mail: nbaoffice@nationalbraille.org
Web: www.nationalbraille.org

National Braille Press
  88 Saint Stephen Street
  Boston, MA 02115
  617.266.6160; 800.548.7323
  E-mail: orders@nbp.org
  Web: www.nbp.org

National Center for Learning Disabilities
  381 Park Avenue South, Suite 1401
  New York, NY 10016.
  888.575.7373; 212.545.7510.
  Web: www.ld.org

National Down Syndrome Congress
  1370 Center Drive, Suite 102
  Atlanta, GA 30338
  800.232.6372; 770.604.9500
  E-mail: info@ndsccenter.org
  Web: www.ndsccenter.org

National Down Syndrome Society
  666 Broadway
  New York, NY 10012
  212.460.9330
  800.221.4602 (Toll Free)
  E-mail: info@ndss.org
  Web: www.ndss.org

National Eye Institute
  31 Center Drive, MSC 2510
  Bethesda, MD 20892-2510
  301.496.5248
  E-mail: 2020@nei.nih.gov
  Web: www.nei.nih.gov

National Federation of the Blind, Parents Division
  1800 Johnson Street
  Baltimore, MD 21230
  410.659.9314, ext. 360
  E-mail: nfb@nfb.org
  Web: www.nfb.org/nopbc.htm

National Institute on Deafness and Other Communication Disorders Information Clearinghouse
  1 Communication Avenue
  Bethesda, MD 20892-3456
  800.241.1044 (V); 800.241.1055 (TTY)
  E-mail: nidcdinfo@nidcd.nih.gov
  Web: www.nidcd.nih.gov/

National Institutes of Health
  Autism Research Network
  Web: www.autismresearchnetwork.org/AN/
  O.A.S.I.S. Online Asperger Syndrome Information and Support
  Web: www.aspergersyndrome.org/

National Information Center for Children and Youth with Disabilities (NICHCY)
  P.O. Box 1492
  Washington, DC 20013-1492
  800.695.0285
  Web: www.nichcy.org

National Institute of Neurological Disorders and Stroke (NINDS)
  National Institutes of Health
  P.O. Box 5801
  Bethesda, MD 20824
  301.496.5751
  800.352.9424
  Web: www.ninds.nih.gov

National Library Service for the Blind and Physically Handicapped
Library of Congress
1291 Taylor Street, NW
Washington, DC 20011
202.707.5100; 202.707.0744 (TTY); 800.424.8567 (Toll Free)
E-mail: nls@loc.gov
Web: www.loc.gov/nls

National Mental Health Association
2001 N. Beauregard Street, 12th Floor
Alexandria, VA 22311
703.684.7722
800.969.6642
800.433.5959 (TTY)
Web: www.nmha.org

National Mental Health Information Center
P.O. Box 42557
Washington, DC 20015
800.789.2647
866.889.2647 (TTY)
Web: www.mentalhealth.org

National Resource Center for Traumatic Brain Injury (NRC TBI)
Department of Physical Medicine and Rehabilitation
P.O. Box 980542
Richmond, VA 23298-0542
804.828.9055
E-mail: mbking@hsc.vcu.edu
Web: www.neuro.pmr.vcu.edu

Prevent Blindness America
500 E. Remington Road
Schaumburg, IL 60173
847.843.2020; 800.221.3004 (Toll Free)
E-mail: info@preventblindness.org
Web: www.preventblindness.org

Professional Development in Autism Center
206.543.4011
Web: http://depts.washington.edu/pdacent/

Recording for the Blind and Dyslexic
20 Roszel Road
Princeton, NJ 08540
866.732.3585; 609.452.0606.
E-mail: custserv@rfbd.org
Web: www.rfbd.org

Research and Training Center on Family Support and Children's Mental Health
Portland State University
P.O. Box 751
Portland, OR 97207-0751
Web: www.rtc.pdx.edu

Schwab Learning
Web: www.schwablearning.org

Self Help for Hard of Hearing People (SHHH)
7910 Woodmont Avenue, Suite 1200
Bethesda, MD 20814
301.657-2248 (V); 301.657.2249 (TTY)
E-mail: info@hearingloss.org
Web: www.hearingloss.org

United Cerebral Palsy Associations, Inc.
1660 L Street NW, Suite 700
Washington DC 20036
800.872.5827 (V/TTY)
202.776.0406 (V)
202.973.7197 (TTY)
Web: www.ucp.org

Yale Child Study Center
Yale Social Learning Disabilities Project
Web: www.autism.fm

Suggested Readings

American Psychiatric Association. *Diagnostic and Statistical Manual of Mental Disorders* (DSM-IV-TR), 4th ed. rev. Washington, DC: American Psychiatric Association, 2000.

Baldi, H., and D. Detmers. *Embracing Play: Teaching Your Child with Autism.* DVD. Bethesda, MD: Woodbine House, 2000 (800-843-7323; www.woodbinehouse.com).

Baldwin, A. Y. "Tests Do Underpredict: A Case Study." *Phi Delta Kappan* 58 (1977): 620–21.

Baldwin, A. Y., and W. Vialle. *The Many Faces of Giftedness: Lifting the Mask.* Albany, NY: Delmar, 1998.

Balter, A. *Coping with Learning Disabilities: A Book for Parents.* Dubuque, IA: Kendall Hunt, 1996.

Barkley, R. *A New Look at ADHD: Inhibition, Time and Self-Control.* DVD. New York: Guilford, 2000.

Barkley, R. *Taking Charge of AD/HD: The Complete Authoritative Guide for Parents.* Rev. ed. New York. Guilford, 2000.

Barton, J. M., and W. T. Starnes. "Identifying Distinguishing Characteristics of Gifted and Talented/Learning Disabled Students." *Roeper Review* 12 (1989): 23–29.

Baum S. "An Enrichment Program for Gifted Learning Disabled Students." *Gifted Child Quarterly* 32, no. 1 (1988): 226–30.

Baum, S. *Gifted but Learning Disabled: A Puzzling Paradox* (Eric Document Reproduction Service No. ED 321 484; ERIC Digest # E479). Reston, VA: Council for Exceptional Children, 1990.

Baum, S. "Meeting the Needs of Gifted/Learning Disabled Students: How Far Have We Come?" *Journal of Secondary Gifted Education* 5 (1994): 6–16.

Baum, S. *Twice-Exceptional and Special Populations of Gifted Students.* Thousand Oaks, CA: Corwin Press, 2004.

Baum, S. M., and S. Owen. "High Ability/Learning Disabled Students: How Are They Different?" *Gifted Child Quarterly* 32 (1988): 321–26.

Baum, S., and F. R. Olenchak. "The Alphabet Children: GT, ADHD and More." *Exceptionality* 10, no. 2 (2002): 77–91.

Betts, G. T. *Autonomous Learner Model.* Greenley, CO: ALPS, 1985.

Beytien, A. *Family to Family: A Guide to Living Life When a Child Is Diagnosed with an Autism Spectrum Disorder.* DVD. Higganum, CT: Starfish Specialty Press, 2004.

Bondy, A., and L. Frost. *A Picture's Worth: PECS and Other Visual Communication Strategies in Autism.* Bethesda, MD: Woodbine House, 2002.

Brody, L. E., and C. J. Mills. "Gifted Children with Learning Disabilities: A Review of the Issues." *Journal of Learning Disabilities* 30, no. 3 (1997): 282–97.

Bruey, C. T. *Demystifying Autism Spectrum Disorders: A Guide to Diagnosis for Parents and Professionals.* Bethesda, MD: Woodbine House, 2003.

Cafiero, J. M. *Meaningful Exchanges for People with Autism: An Introduction to Augmentative and Alternative Communication.* Bethesda, MD: Woodbine House, 2005.

Callard-Szulgit, R. *Parenting and Teaching the Gifted.* Lanham, MD: Rowman & Littlefield, 2003.

Callard-Szulgit, R. *Perfectionism and Gifted Children.* Lanham, MD: Rowman & Littlefield, 2003.

Cash, A. "A Profile of Gifted Individuals with Autism: The Twice-Exceptional Learner." *Roeper Review* 22 (1999): 22–27.

Cline, S., and D. Schwartz. *Diverse Populations of Gifted Children: Meeting Their Needs in the Regular Classroom and Beyond.* Upper Saddle River, NJ: Prentice-Hall, 1999.

Council for Exceptional Children. *Making Assessment Accommodations: A Toolkit for Educators.* Reston, VA: Council for Exceptional Children, 2000.

Cunningham, C. *Understanding Down Syndrome: An Introduction for Parents.* 2nd ed. Cambridge, MA: Brookline, 1999.

Cronin, E. M. *Helping Your Dyslexic Child: A Step-by-Step Program for Helping Your Child Improve Reading, Writing, Spelling, Comprehension, and Self-Esteem.* Rocklin, CA: Prima, 1997.

Currie, P. S., and E. M. Wadlington. *The Source for Learning Disabilities*. East Moline, IL: LinguiSystems, 2000.

Davis, H. "Self-Concept Profiles of Gifted Underachievers." Doctoral dissertation, University of Rochester, 1983. *Dissertation Abstracts international* 45, no. 4 (1984): 1072 (University Microfilms International No. AAC84-13056).

DeBoskey, D. S., ed. *Coming Home: A Discharge Manual for Families of Persons with a Brain Injury*. Houston, TX: HDI, 1996.

Delisle, J. *Barefoot Irreverence: A Guide to Critical Issues in Gifted Child Education*. Austin, TX: Prufrock Press, Inc., 2002.

Delisle, J. R. *Guiding the Social and Emotional Development of Gifted Youth: A Practical Guide for Educators and Counselors*. New York: Longman, 1992.

Dendy, S. A. Z. *Teaching Teens with ADD and ADHD: A Quick Reference Guide for Teachers and Parents*. Bethesda, MD: Woodbine House, 2000.

DePompei, R., J. Blosser, R. Savage, and M. Lash. *Special Education: IEP Checklist for a Student with a Brain Injury*. Wolfeboro, NH: L&A Publishing/Training, 1998.

DePompei, R., and B. Cluett. *All about Me!* Wolfeboro, NH: L&A Publishing/Training, 1998.

DePompei, R., and J. Tyler. *Learning and Cognitive Communication Challenges: Developing Educational Programs for Students with Brain Injuries*. Wolfeboro, NH: L&A Publishing/Training, 2004.

DuCharme, R., and T. P. Gullotta, eds. *Asperger Syndrome: A Guide for Professionals and Families*. New York: Springer Publishers, 2004.

Eide, B. L., and F. F. Eide. *The Mislabeled Child: How Understanding Your Child's Unique Learning Style Can Open the Door to Success*. New York: Hyperion, 2006.

Epilepsy Foundation of America. *Epilepsy: Questions and Answers about Seizure Disorders*. Landover, MD: Epilepsy Foundation of America, n.d.

Fowler, M. *Maybe You Know My Kid: A Parent's Guide to Identifying, Understanding, and Helping Your Child with ADHD*. 3rd ed. Kensington, NY: Citadel, 1999.

Fowler, M. *Maybe You Know My Teen: A Parent's Guide to Helping Your Adolescent with Attention Deficit Hyperactivity Disorder*. New York: Broadway, 2001.

Fowler, M. "Attention-Deficit/Hyperactivity Disorder." *NICHCY Briefing Paper* (2002): 1–24.

Freeman, J. M., E. P. G. Vining, and D. J. Pillas. *Seizures and Epilepsy in Childhood: A Guide for Parents*. 3rd ed. Baltimore, MD: Johns Hopkins University Press, 2003.

Gallagher, J. J. "National Agenda for Educating Gifted Students: Statement of Priorities." *Exceptional Children* 55 (1988): 107–14.

Geralis, E. *Children with Cerebral Palsy: A Parents' Guide.* 2nd ed. Bethesda, MD: Woodbine House, 1998.

Glasberg, B. *Functional Behavior Assessment for People with Autism: Making Sense of Seemingly Senseless Behavior.* Bethesda, MD: Woodbine House, 2005.

Goldberg-Edelson, M. "Autism-Related Disorders in DSM-IV." Center for the Student of Autism website, www.autism.org/dms.html (1995).

Grantham, T. C. "Underrepresentation in Gifted Education: How Did We Get Here and What Needs to Change? Straight Talk on the Issue of Underrepresentation: An Interview with Dr. Mary M. Fraiser." *Roeper Review* 24, no. 1 (2002): 50–51.

Green, B. S., K. M. Stevens, and T. D. Wolfe. *Mild Traumatic Brain Injury: A Therapy and Resource Manual.* San Diego, CA: Singular, 1997.

Greene, R. W. *The Explosive Child: A New Approach for Understanding and Parenting Easily Frustrated Chronically Inflexible Children.* New York: Harper Collins, 2001.

Hall, S., and L. C. Moats. *Straight Talk about Reading: How Parents Can Make a Difference During the Early Years.* New York: McGraw Hill/Contemporary, 1998.

Harwell, J. M. *Complete Learning Disabilities Handbook: Ready-to-Use Strategies and Activities for Teaching Students with Learning Disabilities.* 2nd ed. West Nyack, NJ: John Wiley & Sons, 2002.

Henley, M., R. S. Ramsey, and R. Algozzine. *Characteristics of and Strategies for Teaching Students with Mild Disabilities.* Needham Heights, MA: Allyn & Bacon, 1999.

Hibbard, M., W. Gordon, T. Martin, B. Rashkin, and M. Brown. *Students with Traumatic Brain Injury: Identification, Assessment, and Classroom Accommodations.* New York: Research and Training Center on Community Integration of Individuals with Traumatic Brain Injury, 2001.

Holbrook, M. C., ed. *Children with Visual Impairments: A Parents' Guide.* Bethesda, MD: Woodbine, 1996.

Irvine, D. J. "What Research Doesn't Show about Gifted Dropouts." *Educational Leadership* 44 (1987): 79–80.

Jordan, D. *A Guidebook for Parents of Children with Emotional or Behavior Disorders.* 3rd ed. Minneapolis, MN: PACER, 2001.

Karnes, M. B., A. M. Shwedel, and G. F. Lewis. "Long-Term Effects of Early Programming for the Young Gifted Handicapped Child." *Exceptional Children* 50 (1983): 103–9.

Kelker, K. A., and R. Holt. *Family Guide to Assistive Technology.* Cambridge, MA: Brookline Books, 2000.

Koplewicz, H. S. *It's Nobody's Fault: New Hope and Help for Difficult Children.* New York: Three Rivers Press, 1997.

Lash, M., G. Wolcott, and S. Pearson. *Signs and Strategies for Educating Students with Brain Injuries: A Practical Guide for Teachers and Schools.* 2nd ed. Houston, TX: HDI, 2000.

Lechtenberg, R. *Epilepsy and the Family: A New Guide.* 2nd ed. Cambridge, MA: Harvard University Press, 2002.

Lenz, K., and J. Schumaker. *Adapting Language Arts, Social Studies and Science Materials for the Inclusive Classroom: Volume 3: Grades Six through Eight.* Reston, VA: Council for Exceptional Children, 1999.

Lerner, J. W. *Learning Disabilities: Theories, Diagnosis, and Teaching Strategies.* 8th ed. Boston: Houghton Mifflin, 2000.

Lewis, S., and C. B. Allman. *Seeing Eye to Eye: An Administrator's Guide to Students with Low Vision.* New York: American Foundation for the Blind, 2000.

Little, C. "Which Is It? Asperger's Syndrome or Giftedness: Defining the Differences." *Gifted Child Today* (Winter, 2002): 58–63.

Luterman, D. M. *When Your Child Is Deaf: A Guide for Parents.* 2nd ed. Parkton, MD: York Press, 2002.

Lyle, M. *The LD Teacher's IEP Companion: Goals, Strategies, and Activities for LD Students.* East Moline, IL: LinguiSystems, 1998.

Martin, D. L., Jr. *Identifying Potential Dropouts: A Research Report* (ERIC Document Reproduction Service No. ED 216304). Frankfort, KY: Kentucky State Department of Education, 1981.

Maslow, A. H., and R. Lowery, ed. *Toward a Psychology of Being.* 3rd. ed. New York: Wiley & Sons, 1998.

McCoach, D. B., T. J. Kehle, M. A. Bray, and D. Siegle. "Best Practices in the Identification of Gifted Students with Learning Disabilities." *Psychology in the Schools* 38 (2001): 402–11.

Medwid, D. J., and D. C. Weston. *Kid-Friendly Parenting with Deaf and Hard of Hearing Children: A Treasury of Fun Activities Toward Better Behavior.* Washington, DC: Gallaudet University Press, 1995.

Mercer, C. D., and A. R. Mercer. *Teaching Students with Learning Problems.* 6th ed. New York: Prentice Hall College, 2001.

Mesibov, G. B., V. Shea, and E. Schopler. *The TEACCH Approach to Autism Spectrum Disorders.* New York: Springer Publishers, 2004.

Miller, F., and S. J. Bachrach. *Cerebral Palsy: A Complete Guide for Caregiving.* Baltimore, MD: Johns Hopkins University Press, 1998.

Miller, J. A. (1999). *The Childhood Depression Sourcebook.* New York: McGraw-Hill.

Moon, S. M., S. S. Zentall, J. A. Grskovic, A. Hall, and M. Stormont-Spungin. "Emotional, Social and Family Characteristics of Boys with AD/HD and Giftedness: A Comparative Case Study." *Journal for the Education of the Gifted* 24 (2001): 207–47.

National Association for Gifted Children. *Students with Concomitant Gifts and Learning Disabilities* (NAGC Position Paper). Washington, DC: National Association for Gifted Children, 1998.

National Center for Education Statistics. *Dropout Rates in the United States:* (NCES 98-250). Washington DC: U.S. Government Printing Office, 1997.

National Eye Institute. *Eye Health Organizations List.* Bethesda MD: National Eye Institute, 2003.

National Institutes of Health. "Diagnosis and Treatment of Attention Deficit Hyperactivity Disorder." *NIH Consensus Statement* 16, no. 2 (1998): 1–37.

Neihart, M. "Gifted Children with Asperger's Syndrome." *Gifted Children Quarterly* 44, no. 4 (2000): 222–30.

Nielsen, M. E. "Gifted Students with Learning Disabilities: Recommendations for Identification and Programming." *Exceptionality* 10 (2002): 93–111.

Nugent, M. J. *Handbook on Dual Diagnosis.* Evergreen, CO: Mariah Management, 1998.

O'Brien, M., and J. A. Daggett. *Beyond the Autism Diagnosis: A Professional's Guide to Helping Families.* Baltimore, MD: Brookes Publishing, 2006.

Ogden, P. W. *The Silent Garden: Raising Your Deaf Child.* Rev. ed. Washington, DC: Gallaudet University Press, 1996.

Papolos, D., and J. Papolos. *The Bipolar Child.* New York: Broadway, 2002.

Porterfield, K. M. *Straight Talk about Learning Disabilities.* New York: Facts on File, 1999.

Pueschel, S. M., ed. *A Parent's Guide to Down Syndrome: Toward a Brighter Future.* 2nd ed. Baltimore, MD: Paul H. Brookes, 2001.

Reis, S. M., and D. B. McCoach. "The Underachievement of Gifted Students: What Do We Know and Where Do We Go?" *Gifted Child Quarterly* 44 (2000): 152–70.

Reis, S. M., J. M. McGuire, and T. W. Neu. "Compensation Strategies Used by High Ability Students with Learning Disabilities Who Succeed in College." *Gifted Child Quarterly* 44, no. 2 (2000): 123–34.

Reis, S. M., T. W. Neu, and J. M. McGuire. "Case Studies of High Ability Students with Learning Disabilities Who Have Achieved." *Exceptional Children* 63 (1997): 463–79.

Richman, S. *Raising a Child with Autism: A Guide to Applied Behavior Analysis for Parents.* London: Jessica Kingsley Publishers, 2000.

Ross, P. *National Excellence: A Case for Developing America's Talent.* Washington, DC: U.S. Government Printing Office, 1993.

Schoenbrodt, L., ed. *Children with Traumatic Brain Injury: A Parents' Guide.* Bethesda, MD: Woodbine House, 2001.

Schwartz, S., ed. *Choices in Deafness: A Parents' Guide to Communication Options.* 2nd ed. Bethesda, MD: Woodbine House, 1996.

Senelick, R. C., and K. Dougherty. *Living with Brain Injury: A Guide for Families.* 2nd ed. San Diego, CA: Singular, 2001.

Silver, L. *The Misunderstood Child: Understanding and Coping with Your Child's Learning Disabilities.* 3rd ed. New York: Three Rivers Press, 1998.

Silver, L. *The Misunderstood Child: A Guide for Parents of Children with Learning Disabilities.* 2nd ed. New York: McGraw-Hill, 1991.

Smith, C., and L. W. Strick. *Learning Disabilities from A to Z.* New York, NY: Simon & Schuster, 1999.

Smith, S. *No Easy Answers.* Rev. ed. New York: Bantam, 1995.

Snyder, H. *Elvin the Elephant Who Forgets.* Wolfeboro, NH: L&A Publishing/Training, 1998.

Sternberg, R. J. *Why Smart People Can Be So Stupid.* New Haven, CT: Yale University Press, 2002.

Sulzer-Azaroff, B., and G. R. Mayer. *Behavior Analysis for Lasting Change.* Fort Worth, TX: Holt Rinehart & Winston, 1991.

Unruh, J. F. *Down Syndrome: Successful Parenting of Children with Down Syndrome.* Eugene, OR: Fern Ridge Press, 1994.

Volkmar, F. R., and L. A. Wiesner. *Healthcare for Children on the Autism Spectrum: A Guide to Medical, Nutritional, and Behavioral Issues.* Bethesda, MD: Woodbine House, 2003.

Webb, J. T., E. R. Amand, N. E. Webb, J. Goerss, P. Beljan, and F. R. Olenchack. *Misdiagnosis and Dual Diagnosis of Gifted Children and Adults: ADHD, Bipolar, OCD, Asperger's, Depression and Other Disorders.* Scottsdale, AZ: Great Potential Press, 2005.

Webb, J. T., and E. R. DeVries. *Gifted Parent Groups: The SENG Model.* Scottsdale, AZ: Great Potential Press, 1998.

Weinfeld, R., L. Barnes-Robinson, S. Jeweler, and B. Shevitz. "Academic Programs for Gifted and Talented/Learning Disabled Students." *Roeper Review* 24 (2002): 226–33.

Wilen, T. E. *Straight Talk about Psychiatric Medications for Kids.* New York: Guilford, 1998.

Wiseman, N. D. *Could It Be Autism?* New York: Broadway Books, 2006.

Wright, J. A. *Supporting Children with Communication Problems: Sharing the Workload.* London: David Fulton, 1998.

~

Glossary

Ability. A characteristic that is indicative of competence in a field.

Ability testing. Use of standardized tests to evaluate an individual's performance in a specific area (e.g., cognitive, psychomotor, or physical functioning).

Accommodations. Changes in format, response, setting, timing, or scheduling that do not alter in any significant way what the test measures or the comparability of scores. Accommodations are designed to ensure that an assessment measures the intended construct, not the child's disability. Accommodations affect three areas of testing: (1) the administration of tests, (2) how students are allowed to respond to the items, and (3) the presentation of the tests (how the items are presented to the students on the test instrument). Accommodations may include Braille forms of a test for blind students or tests in native languages for students whose primary language is other than English.

Achievement test. A standardized test that measures knowledge and skills in academic subject areas. Such tests include the Woodcock-Johnson (revised), WIAT, Key Math, TORC, TOWL, TERA, TEMA, and TEWL.

Adaptation. Modification to the delivery of instruction or materials used with a student.

Age equivalent. The chronological age in a population for which a score is the median (middle) score. If children who are 10 years and 6 months old have a median score of 17 on a test, the score 17 has an age equivalent of 10-6.

Alternative assessment. Usually an alternative to a paper-and-pencil test: refers to nonconventional methods of assessing achievement (e.g., work samples and portfolios).

Aptitude. An individual's ability to learn or to develop proficiency in an area if provided with appropriate education or training. Aptitude tests include tests of general academic (scholastic) ability; tests of special abilities (i.e., verbal, numerical, mechanical); tests that assess "readiness" for learning; and tests that measure ability and previous learning that are used to predict future performance.

Assessment. The process of testing and measuring skills and abilities. Assessments include aptitude tests, achievement tests, and screening tests.

Assistive Technology (AT). A generic term that includes assistive, adaptive, and rehabilitative devices and the progress used in selecting, locating, and using them. AT promotes greater independence for people with disabilities.

Asynchronous Development. An uneven development often associated with gifted children, for example, ability to discuss the problem of world hunger at the age of five conflicting with the emotion of not wanting to go to bed. A gifted child's emotional and social development will not always match his or her intellectual development.

Audio spell check. Computer software that pronounces the word to help with spelling.

Battery. A group or series of tests or subtests; the most common test batteries are achievement tests that include subtests in different areas.

Bell curve. See **normal distribution curve.**

Benchmark. Levels of academic performance used as checkpoints to monitor progress toward performance goals and/or academic standards.

Best Practices. The most efficient and effective ways of accomplishing a task, based on repeatable procedures that have proven themselves over time for large numbers of people.

Categories for individuals identified with disabilities. Areas of disabilities defined by federal/state eligibility criteria: Specific Learning Disabled (SLD); Speech/Language Impaired (SLI); Emotionally Disturbed (ED); Otherwise Health Impaired (OHI), which includes ADD/ADHD, Tourette Syndrome, epilepsy, seizures, diabetes, and other chronic or acute health issues; Autism (A); Traumatic Brain Injury (TBI); Hearing Impaired (HI); Vision Impaired (VI); Mildly Mentally Retarded (MIMR); Moderately Mentally Retarded (MOMR); and Orthopedic Impairment (OI).

Ceiling. The highest level of performance or score that a test can reliably measure.

Classroom assessment. An assessment developed, administered, and scored by a teacher to evaluate individual or classroom student performance.

Competency test. A test that measures proficiency in subject areas like math and English. Some states require that students pass competency tests before graduation from high school.

Composite score. A score combining two or more subtest scores to create an average score. For example, a reading performance score may be an average of vocabulary and reading comprehension subtest scores.

Content area. An academic subject such as math, reading, or English.

Content standards. Expectations about what the child should know and be able to do in different subjects and grade levels; they define expected student skills and knowledge and what schools should teach.

Core curriculum. Fundamental knowledge that all students are required to learn in school.

Criteria. Guidelines or rules that are used to judge performance on criterion-referenced tests, which usually cover relatively small units of content and are closely related to instruction.

Criterion-referenced test. A test in which the individual's performance is compared to an objective or performance standard, not to the performance of other students. Its score has meaning in terms of what the student knows or can do, rather than (or in addition to) their relation to the scores of a norm group. Frequently, the meaning is given in terms of a cutoff score, at or above which the criteria are considered to have been met and the material adequately "mastered."

Curriculum. An instruction plan of skills, lessons, and objectives on a particular subject; it may be authored by a state or a textbook publisher. A teacher typically executes this plan.

Diagnostic test. A test used to diagnose, analyze, or identify specific areas of weakness and strength in order to determine the nature of weaknesses or deficiencies; diagnostic achievement tests are used to measure skills.

Expected growth. The average growth change in test scores that occurs over a specific time for individuals at age or grade levels.

FAPE. Free and appropriate public education.

Floor. The lowest score that a test can reliably measure.

Grade equivalents. Test scores that equate a score to a particular grade level. Example: If a child scores at the average of all fifth graders tested, the child would receive a grade equivalent score of 5.0. Use with caution.

Independent Education Evaluation (IEE). A procedure, test, or other assessment done by a qualified examiner who does not work for the school district or other public agency responsible for the child's education.

Individualized education program (IEP). As per federal law (IDEA part 200.1 t), a written plan that specifies the special education programs and services to be provided to meet the unique educational needs of a student with a disability.

Individuals with Disabilities Education Act (IDEA). Federal law with guidelines that mandate requirements for individuals identified with disabilities. In addition, existing state laws and regulations must continue to be implemented to the extent consistent with federal requirements. Original IDEA was authorized in 1996; the new IDEA was reauthorized in 2004 and had to be implemented by each state by July 1, 2005.

Intelligence quotient (IQ). Score achieved on an intelligence test that identifies learning potential.

Intelligence test. A test that measures aptitude or intellectual capacities. (Examples: Wechsler Intelligence Scale for Children (WISC.III-R) and Standford-Binet (SB:IV).

Interdisciplinary approach. A method of teaching that incorporates two or more academic areas that are usually taught separately, such as combining music, reading, art, and writing.

Intervention. An attempt by a child's classroom teacher, parents, or interested others to resolve a problem the child is having before a referral is made for a full and individual evaluation.

KWL chart. A chart used to record what a student knows, wants to learn, and learns about a specific topic.

Least-restrictive environment. Federal law (34 CFR 300.550) states that each public agency shall insure: (1) that to the maximum extent appropriate, children with disabilities, including children in public or private institutions or other care facilities, are educated with children who are nondisabled, and (2) that special classes, separate schooling, or other removal of children with disabilities form the regular educational environment occurs only when the nature or severity of the disability is such that education in regular classes with the use of supplementary aids and services cannot be achieved satisfactorily.

Mastery level. The cutoff score on a criterion-referenced or mastery test; people who score at or above the cutoff score are considered to have mastered the material; "master" may be an arbitrary judgment.

Mastery test. A test that determines whether an individual has mastered a unit of instruction or skill; a test that provides information about what an individual knows, not how his or her performance compares to the norm group.

Mentors. People who are successful in one or more areas of expertise and who share their time and guidance with gifted children who have a similar interest.

Mnemonic device. A tool such as a formula or rhyme used to aid memory.

Modifications. Changes in the content, format, and/or administration of a test to accommodate test takers who are unable to take the test under standard test conditions. Modifications alter what the test is designed to measure or the comparability of scores.

Multidisciplinary team (M-Team). A team consisting of parents, regular classroom teacher, and special education staff, which may include school psychologist, special ed. teachers, speech/language pathologist, occupational therapist, physical therapist, hearing and vision specialists, school nurse, school administrator, and other district personnel deemed necessary to fully address the student's individual strengths and weaknesses. This team reviews the strategies implemented to date, levels of progress achieved, and other interferences that keep the student from attaining an education within normal achievement levels. They then make a determination if further testing is required and if possible special education services may be appropriate.

Multisensory teaching method. An approach to education in which a child learns through more than one of the senses.

National percentile rank. The relative standing of a child compared with others in the same grade. Percentile ranks range from a low score of 1 to a high score of 99.

Normal distribution curve. A distribution of scores used to scale a test. A normal distribution curve is a bell-shaped curve with most scores in the middle and a small number of scores at the low and high ends.

Norm-referenced test. A standardized test designed to compare children's scores to scores achieved by children the same age who have taken the same test. Most standardized achievement tests are norm-referenced.

Objectives. Stated, desirable outcomes of education.

Organizational software. Computer software that assists students in writing by automatically organizing notes into outline form.

Out-of-level testing. Assessing students in one grade level using versions of tests that were designed for students in other (usually lower) grade levels. The test may not assess the same content standards at the same levels as are assessed in the grade-level assessment.

Percentile or percentile rank (PR). The percentage of scores that fall below a point on a score distribution. For example, a score at the 75th percentile indicates that 75 percent of the students obtained that score or lower.

Performance standards. What a child must do to demonstrate proficiency at specific levels in content standards.

Portfolio. A collection of work that shows progress and learning. It can be designed to assess progress, learning, effort, and/or achievement.

Positive behavior support (PBS). An applied science that uses educational and systems change methods (environmental redesign) to enhance quality of life and minimize problem behavior.

Profile. A graphic representation of an individual's scores on several tests or subtests. It allows for easy identification of strengths or weaknesses across different tests or subtests.

Raw score. The number of questions answered correctly on a test or subtest. For example, if a test had 59 items and the student got 23 items correct, the raw score would be 23. Raw scores are converted to percentile ranks, standard scores, and grade-equivalent and age-equivalent scores.

Reliability. The consistency with which a test measures the area being tested. Reliability describes the extent to which a test is dependable, stable, and consistent when administered to the same individuals on different occasions.

Score. A specific number that results from the assessment of an individual

Self-advocacy. Knowing your rights and understanding your learning disability so that you can ask for the accommodations that you really need.

Standard deviation (SD). A measure of the variability of a distribution of scores. The more the scores cluster around the mean, the smaller the standard deviation. In a normal distribution, 68 percent of the scores fall within one standard deviation above and one standard deviation below the mean.

Standardization. A consistent set of procedures for designing, administering, and scoring an assessment. The purpose of standardization is to ensure that all individuals are assessed under the same conditions and are not influenced by different conditions.

Standards. Statements that describe what students are expected to know and do in each grade and subject area; they include content standards, performance standards, and benchmarks.

Standard score. A score on a norm-referenced test that is based on the bell curve and its equal distribution of scores from the average of the distribution. Standard scores are especially useful because they allow for comparisons between students and comparisons of one student over time.

Strength-based instruction. Teaching that uses methods and strategies in the classroom that allow 2E students to use their strengths to succeed, rather than focusing solely on remediation of a weakness(es).

Subtest. A group of test items that measure a specific area (e.g., math calculation or reading comprehension). Several subtests make up a test.

Task analysis. Determination of all the steps that are required to complete a given work assignment.

Test. A collection of questions that may be divided into subtests that measure abilities in an area or in several areas.

Test bias. The difference in test scores that is attributable to demographic variables (e.g., gender, ethnicity, or age).

Thinking skills. Relatively specific cognitive operations that can be considered the "building blocks" of thinking.

Validity. The extent to which a test measures the skill it sets out to measure and the extent to which inferences and actions made on the basis of test scores are appropriate and accurate.

~

About the Author

Dr. Rosemary Callard-Szulgit has forty years of teaching experience and counseling with gifted children, their parents, and other educators—devoting her entire career to the fair and equitable education of all children.

As an adjunct faculty member at the State University of New York College at Brockport, Rosemary continues with her very popular courses in gifted studies. She was also the former coordinator for gifted studies in a large suburban school district in Rochester, New York. Rosemary has spoken extensively both nationally and internationally and continues her staff development trainings with school districts throughout the United States. She is listed in *Who's Who Among American Educators*.

Dr. Callard-Szulgit has written four other books, *Parenting and Teaching the Gifted; Perfectionism and Gifted Children; Teaching the Gifted in an Inclusion Classroom: Activities That Work*; and *Mind-Bending Math and Science Activities for Gifted Children, Grades K–12*.

Her consulting business, Partners for Excellence, may be accessed on the Internet at www.partners-for-excellence.com.

LaVergne, TN USA
08 November 2010
204044LV00006B/56/P